THE
THREE PRINCIPAL ASPECTS
OF THE PATH

THE
THREE PRINCIPAL ASPECTS
OF THE PATH

An Oral Teaching by Geshe Sonam Rinchen
on Tsongkhapa's *Lam gyi gtso bo rnam gsum*

Translated and Edited by Ruth Sonam

Snow Lion Publications
Ithaca, New York, USA

Snow Lion Publications
P.O. Box 6483
Ithaca, New York 14851 USA
Tel. 607-273-8519

ISBN 1-55939-116-2

Printed in Canada on acid-free, recycled paper.

Library of Congress Cataloging-in-Publication Data

Sonam Rinchen, 1933-
        The three principal aspects of the path : an oral teaching / by
Geshe Sonam Rinchen ; translated and edited by Ruth Sonam.
                p.   cm.
        Commentary on Lam gyi gtso bo rnam gsum by Tsongkhapa;
includes the text in Tibetan.
        Includes bibliographical references.
        ISBN 1-55939-116-2 (alk. paper)
        1. Tsoṅ-kha-pa Blo-bzaṅ-grags-pa, 1357-1419. Lam gyi gtso bo
rnam gsum. 2. Buddhism—Doctrine. 3. Dge-lugs-pa (Sect)—Doctrines.
I. Sonam, Ruth, 1943-   . II. Tsoṅ-kha-pa Blo-bzaṅ-grags-pa, 1357-
1419. Lam gyi gtso bo rnam gsum. III. Title.
BQ7950.T754L358 1999
294.3'923—dc21
                                                                99-25974
                                                                CIP

CONTENTS

ASPIRATION

Homage to Manjushri, as supreme peacemaker, whose sword cuts through ignorance, the source of all conflicts. May there be peace in our hearts and in our world.

ACKNOWLEDGMENT

I would like to thank my editor Susan Kyser for her assistance.

INTRODUCTION

HOW TO APPROACH THE TEACHING

This life in which we enjoy exceptional freedom and fortune is full of meaning, since we can accomplish any purpose we wish, but if we use this precious opportunity only to inflict harm on those we dislike and to take care of our friends and loved ones, we do nothing that distinguishes us from animals. Instead we should extract the essence from our human existence by putting it to good use. The great Indian Bodhisattva Shantideva reminds us of this in *Engaging in the Bodhisattva Deeds*:[1]

> Having gained freedom and fortune,[2] so hard to find,
> With which a person's aims can be accomplished,
> If you do not put them to good use,
> How will you ever meet with them again?

We can learn to make best use of this opportunity by following teachings from an authentic and reliable source through which others have succeeded in gaining insights. With an open heart and mind we should absorb these teachings, reflect on them and integrate them through meditation.

The teachings will help to bring about an inner transformation if we approach them in a constructive way by avoiding three faults and fostering six attitudes. The Buddha said, "Listen well, thoroughly and remember." Listening well entails giving what is said full attention and not being like a pot which has been turned upside down. To listen thoroughly we must be free from polluting intentions which make us like a dirty pot. If we do not take care to keep what we hear in mind, we remember nothing and are like a pot with a hole in it.

No matter how tasty the delicacies or how fragrant and fine the nectar, nothing can enter a pot which is upside down. The fault does not lie with the food or drink but with the pot. When you are physically present but distracted and do not listen to the teachings well, the words and their meaning cannot enter your mind and the purpose of attending teachings will not be accomplished.

No matter what drink is put into a pot with a hole, it will leak out and there will be nothing left to enjoy. Even when you listen carefully and give your attention to what is said, if you forget it afterwards you will not know what to practice and the true purpose of listening to teachings will not have been fulfilled.

A dirty pot spoils whatever is put in it and makes it unusable. You may listen attentively and remember what you have heard, but it will be of no true benefit to you if you are motivated by any of the poisonous disturbing emotions or are concerned only with the well-being of this life. The true purpose of listening to teachings, remembering them and familiarizing ourselves with them is to decrease our attachment, hostility and confusion and to make our mind more peaceful and controlled. With a polluted motivation our involvement with spiritual teachings may simply serve to increase these poisonous emotions.

Being like the pot which is upside down prevents you from developing knowledge derived from hearing the teachings. Being like the pot which leaks stops you gaining knowledge derived from thinking about them, and being like the dirty pot is an obstacle to knowledge attained through meditation, which is how you rid yourself of the disturbing emotions.

To counteract these faults listen to the teachings attentively, try to recall what you have heard repeatedly and remind yourself to arouse a pure intention, such as the wish to be free from cyclic existence or to attain enlightenment for the sake of all living beings. For a true practitioner such a focused approach is necessary not only when listening to teachings but at all times. For instance, when practicing analytical meditation give your full attention to the topic under investigation and when practicing placement meditation remain single-pointedly concentrated on your focal object. Between sessions do not simply forget about what occurred during meditation, and when you sit down to meditate again, take to mind what you contemplated in the previous sessions, adding to it little by little, otherwise it is like forgetting everything you learned in your first year of studies when you enter the second year. In all your activities take care to cultivate a pure intention. By doing this your meditation supports your daily life and your everyday experiences inform your meditation.

It is said that the third fault, that of being like a dirty pot because one is motivated by the three poisonous emotions, the eight worldly concerns or self-interest, is the most difficult to overcome. Cultivating six recommended attitudes helps you to do so and automatically also corrects the other faults.

The first attitude is to consider yourself as a sick person. We normally think we are unwell when we have a headache, a stomach ache or some other physical ailment. Despite constantly experiencing many kinds of general and specific suffering associated with cyclic existence, these pains do not make us think that we are sick.

Whatever position people have in society, whether high or low, whether they are men or women, lay or ordained, they experience innumerable kinds of physical and mental suffering. When you first meet someone, you may be impressed by their smart clothes, their air of affluence or their authority and confidence, but once you get to know them they will tell you about their troubles and sorrows.

The disturbing emotions are the underlying cause of our sickness. The chronic sickness itself consists of the contaminated actions we perform because of these emotions. The resultant suffering is like the pain which is symptomatic of the sickness. If we were not really sick, it would be a distortion to consider ourselves sick, but think about how painful anger and desire are. Wherever we are born in the six realms of existence—as hell beings, hungry spirits, animals, humans, demigods or gods—suffering is unavoidable. A human rebirth is considered favorable and still we experience much suffering. For this reason the Kadampa masters[3] have compared us to an incurable patient, a life-prisoner and a traveller who never reaches his destination. In the case of an ordinary sickness one either eventually recovers or gets worse and dies, but there is no such natural end to our chronic sickness.

The second attitude is to see the spiritual teacher as the physician. When you are seriously ill you consult the best doctor you can find. Do not consider a spiritual teacher as an encumbrance, but try your best to practice his or her instructions and to express your respect and reverence.

The third attitude is to see the teachings as the medicine that can cure you. If the doctor prescribes an effective and expensive medicine, you look after it well because you know its value. The teachings are like such a medicine, so cherish them.

The fourth attitude is to take the treatment in order to get better. If you don't use the medicine but leave it carefully stored in the medicine cabinet, it can't help to cure you. The expiration date will come and go and the medicine will have been of no use to you. It is not enough to listen to and cherish the teachings. Be sure to practice them if you want to cure this disease of the disturbing emotions. The doctor stresses the need to take the full course of treatment because just taking the medicine once or twice will not have a lasting effect. Similarly you must keep practicing steadily if your practice is to be fruitful.

The fifth attitude is to see the enlightened ones as excellent beings. As the Indian master Dharmakirti[4] points out, this entails recognizing that the teachings we practice, whose validity can be proven, have come down to us from the Buddha, an authentic teacher and a totally trustworthy person. Learn to appreciate the Buddha's and your teachers' kindness and warmly express your appreciation.

The sixth attitude is to hold in your heart the wish for the teachings to remain in the world for a long time. You would wish to be able to visit your doctor and take treatment until you are cured and for the same opportunity to be available to others. If you truly value the Buddha's kindness, your efforts to insure that the teachings flourish and remain in the world are a token of your gratitude, since the scriptural teachings and their embodiment in the form of insights are the medicine through which living beings can find well-being and happiness. These ways of making your motivation good are applicable not only when you listen to or study teachings but are relevant to all activities, both spiritual and secular.

A BRIEF BIOGRAPHY OF TSONGKHAPA

Tsongkhapa was born in 1357 in the Tsongkha valley of Amdo province in northeast Tibet. The miraculous events that occurred at his birth aroused the interest of the master Chöje Döndrup Rinchen (Chos rje Don grub rin chen), who had studied and lived in central Tibet and who founded two monasteries in Amdo after his return there. When Tsongkhapa was three this master gave a gift of livestock to his father and requested that he should be put in charge of Tsongkhapa's education. At the age of seven Tsongkhapa went to live with Chöje Döndrup Rinchen, from whom he received many teachings and tantric empowerments. Having learned to read and write with great ease, Tsongkhapa both studied and practiced meditation from a very early age. When he was eight years old he received ordination as a novice monk and was given the name Losang Drakpa (Blo bzang grags pa).

At the age of sixteen Tsongkhapa left Amdo to pursue his quest for knowledge in central and southern Tibet, where he studied with more than fifty prominent teachers. Between 1374 and 1376 he concentrated on the Perfection of Wisdom sutras and on the five treatises of Maitreya along with the many commentaries devoted to them. He gained a rigorous intellectual training and a wide knowledge of both sutra and tantra during this period. Tsongkhapa was already determined to combine scholarship with the practice of both sutra and tantra and he continued to receive tantric empowerments from a number of important masters belonging to different traditions.

He was dedicated to developing the correct understanding of reality and at this time had a significant experience of entering a profound state of meditation during a ceremony when the assembled monks were reciting a Perfection of Wisdom sutra. He remained deeply absorbed long after the ceremony was over and the other monks had left the hall. From his twenty-second year he began to study intensively the works on valid cognition by Dignaga and Dharmakirti and was deeply impressed and moved by the efficacy of Dharmakirti's system of reasoning.

For the next eleven years Tsongkhapa travelled from one monastic college to another deepening his philosophical knowledge and giving teachings. His main teacher and close friend during this period was the Sakyapa (Sa skya pa) master Rendawa Shönu Lodrö (Red mda' ba gZhon nu Blo gros).

At the age of thirty-three he met with the remarkable Lama Umapa (dBu ma pa), who came to Tsang (gTsang)[5] with the intention of studying with Tsongkhapa. Umapa had had a vision of Manjushri, the embodiment of enlightened wisdom, which had changed his life from that of a simple cowherd. As a result of this vision he took up practices related to Manjushri and eventually experienced Manjushri's constant presence.

Lama Umapa became Tsongkhapa's direct line of communication with Manjushri They spent periods of retreat together during which Umapa conveyed to Tsongkhapa Manjushri's advice and responses to questions concerning the correct understanding of reality. Eventually Tsongkhapa himself experienced visions of Manjushri, who bestowed empowerments on him and gave him teachings.

During the winter of 1392-1393 in accordance with Manjushri's instructions he stopped teaching and withdrew from other public activities to concentrate on a period of intense meditation. He was joined by a group of eight carefully chosen students. Living austerely, they began practices for purification and the accumulation of merit, reciting purificatory mantras, making prostrations and offerings of the mandala many hundred thousand times. Tsongkhapa simultaneously continued to study the most important texts dealing with the nature of reality.

In 1394 he and the others moved to Wölka ('Ol kha)[6] and while they were there they all experienced visions of deities associated with the practices in which they were engaged. In 1395 they decided to break this retreat to refurbish and reconsecrate a famous and venerated statue of the future Buddha Maitreya which had fallen into disrepair. This generated much interest and many craftsmen and benefactors offered their help for the project, which was successfully completed.

For the next three years Tsongkhapa and his companions continued to practice in Lodrak (lHo brag)[7] and then in 1397 they began a final year of retreat again in the Wölka area. In the late spring of 1398 these concerted and extraordinary efforts finally bore fruit. One night Tsongkhapa dreamed that he was present at a gathering of famous Indian masters discussing the subtleties of the Madhyamika view. One of them, who was dark-skinned and tall and whom Tsongkhapa recognized in the dream as Buddhapalita,[8] rose and, holding a volume in his hands, approached Tsongkhapa and joyfully blessed him by touching his head with the book. Tsongkhapa

woke as it was getting light and opened his own Tibetan translation of Buddhapalita's commentary at the page which he
had been reading the day before. When he reread the passage he at once experienced a seminal insight into the nature
of reality, which brought him the understanding that he had
been seeking.

Among Tsongkhapa's many beneficial activities four are
mentioned in particular. The first was the renovation of the
statue of Maitreya and the subsequent great festival he orga-
nized during the Tibetan New Year in 1400 at Dzingji ('Dzing
ji) temple, which housed the statue. The second was an extensive teaching on the code of discipline for the ordained
which he, Rendawa and Kyapchok Pel Zangpo (sKyabs
mchog dPal bzang po) gave for several months at Namtse
Deng (gNam rtse ldeng), thereby revitalizing the tradition of
monasticism.

The third deed was his establishment of the Great Prayer
Festival in Lhasa in 1409, beginning a tradition that has continued until now of devoting the first two weeks of the Tibetan new year, culminating on the day of the full moon, to
prayers for universal well-being. Tsongkhapa donated everything he himself had received from benefactors to support
this event and offered ornaments made of gold and precious
stones to the famous statue of the Buddha in the main temple
in Lhasa.

The fourth deed was the construction of Ganden Monastery (dGa' ldan) near Lhasa. "Ganden" means "The Joyous"
and is the Tibetan name given to the pure land of Maitreya.
The monastery was completed and consecrated in 1410. In
1415 special halls were built to house selected mandalas.
Under Tsongkhapa's guidance skilled craftsmen created these
mandalas and images of the relevant deities, which were in-
stalled in 1417. All of this was destroyed after the Chinese
occupation of Tibet in 1959.

During his last years Tsongkhapa devoted much of his
energy to giving extensive teachings. He passed away in 1419.
Personally and through his students he made an extremely

significant impact on the development of Buddhism in Tibet and his influence extended to Mongolia and China. He wrote prolifically and lucidly on topics connected with both sutra and tantra and thanks to his clear and elegant style these great works remain illuminating, relevant and accessible to this day.[9]

THE IMPORTANCE OF THE *THREE PRINCIPAL ASPECTS OF THE PATH*

Tsongkhapa's *Three Principal Aspects of the Path*[10] is a summation of all the paths of practice which lead to enlightenment. It is said that Manjushri himself gave the title to this short text. The Buddha's many different teachings were intended to enable us to reach nirvana, the state of liberation from the bonds of disturbing emotions and the contaminated actions they cause, as well as from the resultant suffering associated with cyclic existence. Without an aversion to cyclic existence, especially to all its wonders which hold us in thrall, we cannot free ourselves. There is a glaring discrepancy between what we do and what we say, since we secretly cling tightly to our dreams of these marvels while insisting that we want to gain liberation.

Many factors are necessary for us to free ourselves but the essential prerequisite is a strong wish for freedom. To gain liberation we must cut through the very root of cyclic existence, which is possible only with the correct understanding of reality. Furthermore, while we may feel an antipathy to this cycle of involuntary birth and death and gain an undistorted understanding of reality, we will never attain supreme enlightenment without the altruistic intention to do so for the good and happiness of all living beings.

These three principal paths of insight encapsulate the practices pertaining to persons of three levels of capacity.[11] There are diverse ways of presenting teachings on the stages of the path but the fundamental subject-matter remains the same. All practices relating to the insights of the initial and intermediate levels concern an understanding of the unsatisfactory

and painful nature of cyclic existence and the development
of a wish for freedom. They are therefore subsumed in the
first of the principal paths, the wish to emerge from cyclic
existence.

When we have fully understood our own plight, strong
empathy will easily arise for other living beings who are
embroiled in suffering for the same reasons and who fail to
find the happiness they desire. A person of great capacity
cultivates love, compassion and supreme altruism, which are
included in the second of the principal paths, the altruistic
intention to become enlightened for the welfare of all living
beings.

Our work for others will not be of true benefit unless we
can discern what they need and how to help them. If what
we do counteracts both the obstacles formed by the disturbing emotions, which prevent freedom, and the obstructions
to knowledge of all phenomena, we are employing effective
means, otherwise we are not. All the difficulties living beings face spring from ignorance. Those of both the intermediate and great levels of capacity cultivate the correct understanding of reality.

Thus the practices of all three levels are included within
the three principal paths. Listening to, thinking about and
meditating on teachings concerning these three is therefore
like listening to, thinking about and putting into practice all
the Buddha's teachings. If we are truly intent on enlightenment, it is intelligent to direct our attention to the essentials.

These three principal insights are the indispensable support for all the practices of sutra and tantra. We cannot say
that certain people need to cultivate them and others do not,
since the development of these insights would enrich everyone. The fact that most people are not open even to a discussion of such ideas is a different matter. Ask yourself to what
extent you genuinely wish to develop these insights.

Why are these three paths considered essential? Because
they lead us to both the temporary and ultimate happiness
we desire. By following them we will find everything we

need. Any positive action supported by the wish to emerge from cyclic existence, even simply giving a handful of food to an animal, becomes a cause for lasting happiness and for liberation from suffering. If such an action is underlain by the wish to gain enlightenment for the sake of all living beings, it acts as a cause for omniscience, and accompanied by the correct understanding of reality, it is an antidote to cyclic existence.

You may receive tantric initiations and practice sincerely, reciting thousands of mantras in the hope of gaining extraordinary powers or becoming an effective healer. This can indeed bring results, but unless you are motivated by any of these three principal insights, the outcome will be limited and your practice lacks authenticity from a Buddhist standpoint. It will have little connection with what is discussed here.

Many Tibetans recite the mantra *OM MANI PADME HUNG*[12] to avoid taking a bad rebirth. Others say the mantra making fervent requests to Avalokiteshvara because they have heard that this can do wonders for one's eyesight and their vision may well improve. In Tibet I knew several old ladies of whom it was said that they had grown a new tooth by reciting one billion *MANI*s. I was too shy to go up to them and ask to look in their mouths, so I missed a chance to acquire first-hand evidence!

Prostrations are frequently recommended to eliminate poison from the body or to get rid of tumors and it is said that circumambulations help to cure ailments affecting the legs. Done for such reasons these practices are not authentic. Though they may help to heal one, they have been performed merely for the sake of this decaying body. Examine your reasons for listening to the teachings and for going on pilgrimage and to places of practice.

If what you do is motivated by these three positive states of mind, it becomes a cause for liberation and enlightenment. If it isn't, it does not. Without them as the motivating force your negative actions lead to a bad rebirth, your positive actions to a birth as a human or celestial being and your unfluctuating actions to a rebirth in the form and formless realms.[13] Meditation on the energy channels, energy winds and constituents which make up the subtle body and cultivation of the stages of generation and completion[14] will simply act as causes for further rebirth within cyclic existence and will not be genuine practices of tantra.

The Kadampa master Geshe Puchungwa asked another Kadampa master, Geshe Chengawa,[15] which he would choose: mastery of the five different fields of knowledge,[16] steady meditative stabilization, the five kinds of super-knowledge[17] and the eight common powerful attainments[18] or, even without developing the actual insights, gaining a firm and unshakable conviction in Atisha's instructions contained in the *Lamp for the Path to Enlightenment.*[19]

Geshe Chengawa respectfully replied that never mind developing the actual insights described by Atisha, he would prefer even a partial and cursory understanding of the stages of the path to the numerous abilities mentioned by Geshe Puchungwa. He explained that though he had possessed all these accomplishments many times in the past, they had never enabled him to escape from cyclic existence, whereas he felt convinced that insight into the stages of the path set forth by Atisha would certainly help him to gain freedom.

Much later, when Tsongkhapa wrote his *Great Exposition of the Stages of the Path,*[20] he said that these three most important insights formed its mainstay and that it elucidated and expanded on the subject-matter of Atisha's *Lamp for the Path to Enlightenment.*

Manjushri told Tsongkhapa that those who sincerely wish to practice should constantly bear in mind the many disadvantages of this involuntary cycle of existences and the great benefits of gaining liberation. Putting an end to their enthrallment with appearances, they should concentrate on their objective and arouse the wish for freedom. Without this wish, the practices of generosity, ethical discipline, patience, effort and concentration cannot act as causes for liberation, so for the time being they would be wise to leave aside all other instructions and focus their entire energy on arousing the wish to extricate themselves from cyclic existence.

Concern for settling scores and taking care of family and friends and the conviction that getting the best of whatever we desire will bring satisfaction reveals our addiction to what we consider the good things of this life. With such tunnel vision we are unable to tolerate anything that thwarts our aims and even a small slight or cutting remark requires retaliation. All this keeps us so busy that there is no time for spiritual practice.

Failing to appreciate the true significance of this precious human life, we constantly delay spiritual practice because of other issues which seem more pressing. Fascination with this life prevents us from practicing purely. When our fascination is directed towards the good things we hope for in future lives, though our practice of virtue may be genuine because it takes the well-being of future rebirths into consideration, it cannot act as a cause for liberation.

True Mahayana practitioners must remain constantly aware of the faults of selfishness and the great benefits of concern for others. Recognizing the value of cherishing others, they set aside their interest in tantra for the time being and concentrate their energies on gaining personal experience of the altruistic intention, without which their practice of virtue is not a Mahayana activity. When this supreme intention has been developed, everything they do becomes a cause for enlightenment. We should therefore not underestimate the importance of the wish to gain freedom from cyclic existence nor of the altruistic intention.

Criticism of self-interest does not imply that concern for our own well-being is unjustified and inappropriate. But until now this has been our sole focus, and if our single-minded pursuit of it were the way to avoid suffering and find happiness, we should have accomplished our aim long ago. In fact egocentricity kills our chances of happiness now and of liberation and enlightenment in the future.

When the well-being of others is mentioned, "others" refers not just to human beings but to all other living creatures. Their well-being is a state of happiness in which they are free from suffering. The paradox is that if we devote ourselves wholeheartedly to helping others achieve that state, all our own needs will be met in the process.

The Kadampa masters, famed for their pithy comments, said that we so-called practitioners all have a deity for meditation and mantras to recite but nothing happens because the thought of the teachings is not in our hearts. First we must induce our mind to turn to the Buddha's teachings and then arouse a wish for freedom. Next we must insure that our practice of the teachings becomes a true Mahayana path by developing the altruistic intention. Then, by gaining a correct understanding of reality we combat the obstructions to liberation and to perfect enlightenment which are all rooted in our ignorance of how things actually exist.

THE
THREE PRINCIPAL ASPECTS
OF THE PATH

PROLOGUE

RELATING TO THE SPIRITUAL TEACHER

Tsongkhapa begins this short work by offering praise and homage so as to create the auspicious circumstances that will allow him successfully to complete the task in hand.

Homage to the venerable and holy teachers!

His obeisance, not to one but to many teachers, may be taken as an expression of veneration for all his personal mentors, from those who taught him to read and write to those who gave him the profoundest philosophical instruction. From a Buddhist point of view all our teachers are esteemed because of their kindness in imparting knowledge to us. His homage may also be directed to all the spiritual teachers of the extensive deeds lineage, of the profound view lineage and of the inspiring practice lineage.[1]

Tsongkhapa's deep reverence for Manjushri as a personal teacher is apparent from the fact that in many other works he explicitly pays homage to Manjushri. In his *Essence of Good Explanations Regarding the Interpretable and Definitive*[2] he says:

> Many who have heard the treatises extensively,
> Who also strenuously employed many lines of reasoning
> And whose qualities of insight were not inferior,

Despite their efforts failed to understand that which I
Have seen well through the kindness of my teacher,
Manjughosha, and which with great affection I shall explain.

In the past many failed to understand the nature of reality, despite their great learning, prowess in logic and philosophy and despite their numerous beneficial activities. Tsongkhapa attributes the fact that he succeeded to Manjushri's great kindness and, out of profound affection for others, wishes to pass on what he has understood.

Tsongkhapa had frequent visions of Manjushri. I believe in the existence of authentic visionary experiences, accounts of which are found in all spiritual traditions. The reason why most of us do not have such visions is because our minds are clouded by impurity and karmic obstructions. There are different kinds of visions. Great teachers may appear in our dreams and give us instruction. They may also appear and teach us during our meditation. In some cases the vision remains accessible until the teaching has been written down. The third kind of vision is a direct appearance to mental perception or to the senses. This kind of vision is extremely vivid and like an actual meeting. Manjushri appeared to Tsongkhapa's senses.

In discussing how to develop the altruistic intention, we will see that Chandrakirti pays homage to compassion in his *Supplement to the Middle Way.*[3] In the *Ornament for Clear Realizations*[4] Maitreya pays homage to the three kinds of understanding. He says:

> I pay homage to the mothers of the assembly of Hearers, Bodhisattvas and Buddhas—to the knower of all which leads the Hearers who seek peace to pacification; to the knower of paths through which those who help living beings accomplish their well-being; and to that through the possession of which Subduers give diverse teachings on all aspects.[5]

Here Tsongkhapa chooses to pay homage to spiritual teachers because without them we can develop neither great nor small insights, but with their help we can first develop and then strengthen and enhance the three principal realizations discussed here.

Geshe Potowa[6] stressed the importance of the relationship with a spiritual teacher if we wish to gain liberation, reminding us that a teacher is needed even for ordinary secular activities. We have just emerged from bad rebirths and are entering unknown territory in which we need the help of a guide. The spiritual teacher we choose should be capable of teaching us the complete path. If you are learning to draw, you look for a well-qualified teacher, who is an experienced, accomplished and versatile artist. If your teacher is skilled at drawing only faces, what you can learn will necessarily be limited.

Most of us understand the books of Buddhist teachings that we read, but this is not enough. No one has ever gained, nor will ever gain, a state of high realization without guidance from a spiritual teacher. If the mold is good, what is made with it turns out well, while a defective mold can only produce something incomplete. The mentor is like a mold that forms the student and the student comes to resemble him or her, so we must know what to look for in a spiritual teacher. However, the student too must possess certain essential qualities. When a teacher and student who both possess the necessary qualities come together, the alchemical process of transformation can begin.

Various versions of the qualities the mentor should possess are found in different texts, but since we are concerned with teachings of the Great Vehicle here, we can refer to Maitreya's *Ornament for the Mahayana Sutras*[7] in which he lists ten features that provide valuable guidelines. He says:

> The spiritual teacher is subdued, calm, very peaceful,
> With surpassing qualities, persevering, rich in learning,
> With understanding of suchness, skilled in communication,
> Compassionate, undiscouraged and steadfast.

Ideal spiritual teachers are disciplined not simply in their physical and verbal actions but also in their mental activity. They achieve this by observing the three kinds of vows—the personal liberation vow, the Bodhisattva vow and the tantric vow[8]—and by avoiding activities which are contrary to these vows. They are calm because their training in concentration prevents distraction and stops the manifestation of disturbing emotions. They are very peaceful because their training in wisdom thoroughly pacifies these disturbing emotions. Their good qualities and knowledge surpass those of the student in matters regarding which the student seeks guidance. If the teacher's knowledge is inferior or equal to the student's, the student's good qualities will not increase and may decline.

These exemplary mentors teach with untiring enthusiasm and perseverance. They are rich in scriptural knowledge regarding the three categories of teaching.[9] They understand suchness, the final mode of existence, either directly or by way of a mental image or through correct supposition. They should at least have a sound understanding of scriptural texts and reasoning relating to the topic. They are skilled in communicating the teachings clearly in ways appropriate to the student's disposition and are motivated not by the wish for material gain, but by compassion for their students' suffering and lack of happiness. They are undiscouraged by ingratitude or by their students' obstinacy but are patient and steadfast in teaching and guiding them.

It is rare to find spiritual teachers with all these qualities, but your teacher should at least possess some of them. Not only should you ascertain that your potential teacher possesses the knowledge you seek, you must also be convinced of his or her trustworthiness and that you could enter into an enduring relationship with that person. Your teacher should be more interested in spiritual than in secular matters, since this will encourage you to follow suit; more concerned about future lives than about this life and intent on helping students rather than on accumulating wealth or becoming well-known.

As for the students, Aryadeva outlines their prerequisite qualities in his *Yogic Deeds of Bodhisattvas*[10] when he says:

> An unprejudiced, intelligent and interested
> Listener is called a vessel.
> Neither the teacher's nor the student's
> Good qualities will be taken as faults.

Promising students are open-minded and unprejudiced. They are not attached to their own views or culture nor are they hostile to others' views. Their intelligence allows them to differentiate between valuable instructions and those which only appear good. If in addition to this they are enthusiastic and persevering it bodes well for their progress.

Without intelligence you may mistake your teacher's and fellow-students' good qualities for faults or vice versa. Even if you have the intelligence to perceive your teacher's and fellow-students' positive qualities correctly, prejudice may prevent you from admitting the truth. Prejudice is a great hindrance to understanding reality and attaining the peace of nirvana. Without true interest and the enthusiasm to translate what you learn into practice, intelligence and lack of bias are of limited value. You also need respect and faith.

If you want to teach others or to be the student of a spiritual teacher, you should examine yourself to see whether you meet these criteria. If you don't, you can take steps to change. Having found a spiritual teacher, you must create the right kind of relationship. Constantly remind yourself of the numerous advantages this brings and of the many disadvantages of not having a spiritual mentor. Through this relationship you come closer to enlightenment and please all the Victorious Ones. Not cultivating such a relationship or doing so in the wrong way seriously prejudices your spiritual development.

The relationship is cultivated in thought and in deed. To foster it in thought, arouse feelings of faith and respect by thinking about your spiritual teacher's kindness. The great yogi Milarepa[11] said, "Most people's faith is on their lips, but mine, the yogi's, is in my heart." Your faith should be in the very marrow of your bones. Asanga's *Compendium of Knowledge*[12] defines faith as follows:

> What is faith? Conviction in that which exists, appreciation for that which has qualities and the wish for that which has power [to yield the desired result] act as a basis for aspiration.

The faith of conviction arises when you are convinced that what the Buddha said, for instance regarding the fact that virtue gives rise to happiness and not suffering, is true and trustworthy. The feeling is compared to a child's trust in its mother.

Seeing the good qualities of your spiritual teacher and of those in whom you take refuge, you feel appreciative and inspired, which makes your mind clear and ready to develop good qualities. Most of the time one's mind is like muddy water. The faith of appreciation settles the mud of the disturbing emotions, so that the mind becomes bright and limpid. The feeling is compared to the experience of seeing a person with whom you are in love.

The faith of wishing strongly to practice arises when you realize that by overcoming your preoccupation with the good things of this life, by taking refuge repeatedly and gaining conviction in the connection between actions and their effects, you can avoid bad rebirths. The desire to practice also arises when you understand that by overcoming your fascination with the good things associated with future lives and by training yourself in ethical discipline, concentration and wisdom, you can gain freedom from cyclic existence. A further incentive to practice is the realization that by overcoming self-interest and training yourself in the six perfections, you can rid yourself of the obstructions to liberation and enlightenment. This kind of faith is founded on the recognition that these practices have the power to yield their respective results and that you have the capacity to accomplish them. The feeling is like that of a thirsty person looking for water.

Faith is the prerequisite for developing all paths of insight and well-being. All three kinds of faith are essential in creating a good relationship with your spiritual teacher. Imagining your spiritual teacher before you, think again and again that despite looking ordinary, he or she is a Buddha embodying all enlightened beings. By doing this the clear faith of appreciation arises.

However, just regarding your teacher's physical body as a Buddha's will not keep you from perceiving faults. You must recognize his or her good qualities and appreciate them. Devadatta, the Buddha's erring cousin, who caused a schism in the spiritual community that had gathered around the Buddha, could see the Buddha's radiance and the thirty-two major and eighty minor distinguishing features[13] that made him enthralling to behold, but this did not stop him from constantly criticizing the Buddha for imaginary faults.

Repeatedly contemplating the Buddha's statements that everything good, both worldly and supramundane, is the result of your spiritual teacher's kindness and examining your own experience gives rise to the faith of conviction. The faith of aspiration is aroused by reminding yourself that if you wish to attain the enlightened state of your teacher, you need to make enthusiastic effort to practice what he or she instructs you to do.

The Array of Trunks Sutra[14] mentions nine attitudes to foster when mentally cultivating the relationship with a spiritual teacher. These will clearly also affect your actions. The first is to have the attitude of a good child who is obedient to its parents and does not act independently. Give up your independence and do what your spiritual teacher asks of you. Your actions will thereby never be contrary to his or her wishes. By following your spiritual teacher in this way you will always have a teacher in future lives. This may sound highly controversial and risky but actually presents no problems, if you have taken care to seek out a spiritual teacher with the prerequisite qualities. However, the texts contain strong warnings not to let just anyone lead you by the nose, so be intelligent and prudent.

The second is the adamantine attitude of never relinquishing the loving bond you have formed with your teacher. Make your relationship to him or her steadfast and unchanging and allow neither demons nor bad friends to cast a shadow between you. You and your spiritual teacher act as mutually helpful friends, accepting the responsibility to assist each other, but you also become loving friends who can trust and confide in one another. Loving friendships of this kind are rare.

The third is the earth-like attitude. Just as the earth supports everything animate and inanimate without any discouragement, a good student willingly carries all burdens without feeling disheartened.

The fourth describes how to carry these burdens in terms of six attitudes. With a mountain-like attitude you remain firm and unswayed, no matter how difficult or troublesome the tasks are that you have been asked to perform. For instance, you may meet a well-qualified teacher and receive Mahayana teachings, after which you remain nearby to practice, but the place or the food may not be to your liking or even may not agree with you and you feel like leaving. At that time, remember how rare and fortunate it is to find such a teacher and to receive such teachings and try to remain unswayed by the difficulties.

Once the Kadampa master Geshe Potowa told the monks who served Geshe Chengawa, "You are so fortunate to have the opportunity to serve my spiritual master, the Bodhisattva Chengawa. Never consider it a burden but regard it as an adornment because it brings you great merit." If you are wearing a rich brocade robe and marvelous heavy gold jewelry, you regard them as an adornment and never consider their weight, but if these same things are parcelled up and you have to carry them, you think of them as a burden. Reflect on how lucky you are to have found a spiritual teacher, rather than considering the relationship as a restriction.

With a slave-like attitude you willingly carry out lowly tasks without feeling demeaned. This does not, however, imply that you become your teacher's slave. On a particular occasion when Atisha and his disciple Dromtönpa were travelling in Tsang, the only place they could find to spend the night was damp and muddy. Dromtönpa at once took off his sheepskin coat and set to work clearing away the mud and covering the damp patches with dry earth. When he had cleaned and tidied everything and made it as wholesome as he could, he set up a mandala in front of his master. Atisha was surprised and moved by Dromtönpa's behavior and thought to himself, "I've never had such a devoted disciple," but he said, "I used to have a disciple just like you in India."

With a sweeper's attitude you are free from pride and don't consider yourself a big shot. Learn to take the lowest seat. Sometimes the spiritual teacher is modest and the student is puffed up with pride. Once Dromtönpa's student Sherap Yungdrung, known as Geshe Lhabchungwa, arrived very grandly to visit him, accompanied by more than thirty of his own students. Dromtönpa told him, "The water of good qualities will run off the ball of pride called Sherap Yungdrung." And Geshe Chengawa said to his students, "If you look to see where the grass grows first in spring, in the valleys or on the mountain tops, you'll see it grows first in the low-lying areas." Good qualities and insights develop quickly in someone who can adopt a humble position.

With the attitude of a vehicle you willingly carry any responsibilities, no matter how heavy. With a dog-like attitude you don't become downhearted, even if your spiritual teacher scolds you. When you scold or even slap your dog, he comes back after a little while, wagging his tail in a friendly way. Every time Geshe Lhaso went to visit his teacher, Geshe Tölungpa, his teacher reprimanded and found fault with him. One day Geshe Lhaso's student Nyokmopa remarked, "Geshe Tölungpa is always so nasty to us when we go to visit him." Geshe Lhasowa replied, "Is that how you see it? Each time I go there I feel I'm receiving blessings from Heruka."[15]

And finally with a ferry-like attitude you will never feel weary no matter how many times your teacher sends you back and forth on errands.

Atisha was considered the crown jewel of all the great Buddhist scholars and sages of his time. His beneficial influence both within India and in Tibet, his many excellent qualities and the unequalled number of his followers are all attributed to the excellent relationship he had with his spiritual teachers. He could never utter Dharmakirti of Suvarna-dvipa's[16] name without adding words of praise, and whenever that master was mentioned, Atisha rose to make prostrations, shed many tears and spoke of his great kindness. When questioned about this Atisha replied, "I don't possess any exceptional qualities, but whatever small degree of altruism I have is due to his inestimable kindness."

Of Atisha's many students in India and Tibet, Dromtönpa was his true spiritual son. One day some of Atisha's Tibetan students met to discuss who would be his spiritual heir. Gompa Rinchen Lama thought that it would surely be him, since Naktso Lotsawa[17] was Atisha's secretary and Dromtönpa Atisha's attendant. Kutön Tsöndru thought he should be the one because of his great knowledge and brilliance. But Kawa Shakya Wangchuk spoke up and said, "It won't be any of you clever ones but Dromtönpa, who has heard every teaching our master Atisha has given." Then Gompa Rinchen Lama, who was outspoken, protested that he too had heard everything Atisha had taught. He went to Atisha to report what had occurred and forthrightly asked him why Dromtönpa should be his heir. Atisha answered, "I have blessed him." This was not a mark of favoritism, for he had blessed them all equally, but Dromtönpa's complete devotion had opened his heart to receive Atisha's blessings.

The great yogi Milarepa studied black magic in his youth and wreaked much destruction, bringing death to more than thirty people when he caused the roof of his uncle's house to collapse in revenge for his cruelty to Mila and his mother. He damaged fields of crops and killed animals with the hailstorms he caused, but when he met the great translator Marpa, he practiced what this master taught him and in that very life accomplished the highest attainments. He is remembered and admired for his extraordinary devotion to Marpa.

Whether you are near or far away, you can cultivate the relationship with your spiritual teachers by stopping critical thoughts and appreciating their good qualities, by remembering their kindness and by following their instructions. Unless you do this, you will not be performing "guruyoga," no matter how strenuously you visualize your teacher and recite devotional verses. Remind yourself of this important relationship by imagining your principal spiritual teacher on the crown of your head or at your heart.

Milarepa had no material possessions but offered Marpa his wholehearted practice. He said, "When I am among many, I recall my teacher." He also said:

> At times my teacher appears to me,
> And when my teacher appears to me,
> I at once imagine him on my crown
> And make requests from the depths of my heart.

When formally cultivating the relationship with your teachers, imagine them all before you, even those who taught you to read and write. Don't omit the teachers you disliked nor those whom you think taught you nothing important. Our teachers are the root of all blessings. In the tantras the Buddha said that during the time of degeneration when the teachings were in decline, accomplished practitioners would disappear like the stars at dawn. Yet we should not feel discouraged because he himself would appear as spiritual teachers to instruct us on what to practice and what to discard according to our needs and fortune. We should have faith that it is really he and with respect practice the teachings we receive.

Once when Milarepa and Rechungpa were staying in Nyanang[18] to meditate, a group of local people brought them gifts of food. Rechungpa received a great deal and thought Mila must have received even more, so he went to Mila and said, "We have received so many gifts. Let's hold an offering feast for the other meditators." Mila said, "That's fine. The gifts I received are over there on that slate." Rechungpa was shocked to see a very meager collection of gifts. The people had given more generously to Rechungpa because they were impressed by the fact that he had made the long and difficult journey to India, while Mila had not.

Rechungpa felt awkward about this and thought that he was not suitable as Mila's attendant. He had long wanted to make a pilgrimage to central Tibet and so he requested Mila for leave to go. A long discussion ensued because Mila had vowed never to let him go away again, but Rechungpa was so insistent that Mila finally consented.

On his travels Rechungpa started living with a woman he met. Mila came to know of this and recognizing that Rechungpa's great potential to serve the teachings and help them flourish would go to waste, he decided to free his disciple from this entanglement. He emanated a ragged beggar, who arrived at Rechungpa's door. Rechungpa, who was very kindhearted, gave the beggar a large and very fine turquoise. His companion discovered what had happened just as they were about to sit down to eat and was so incensed, she struck him on the head with the soup-ladle she was holding. Rechungpa wryly exclaimed, "I have received many initiations but never a ladle initiation!" Not long after this he left and travelled to where Mila was staying. On reaching the place he went to his teacher and to his enormous surprise saw the very turquoise he had given the beggar in his teacher's hand. At that moment he knew Mila had engineered the appearance of the beggar and all that followed.

Pänchen Losang Chökyi Gyeltsen[19] had a student called Trungpa Gyeltsap[20] who had been trying unsuccessfully to gain certain insights by meditating on the stages of the path. One night a thief came and tied him up tightly to a stone pillar in his house. That night Trungpa Gyeltsap suffered a lot of pain and extreme cold. His suffering triggered many new insights and when he finally was able to get free, he went straight to his teacher's house to tell him about them. Before he could say a word, Pänchen Losang Chökyi Gyeltsen, looking delighted, gave him a thumbs-up sign and said, "Was your mind as hard as stone before?" In a flash Trungpa understood the truth about the thief.

Just as the best and cleanest water comes from mountain snow, the spiritual teacher is the source of good qualities. If you cut off the source, that pure clear water cannot reach you. Similarly without a spiritual teacher you cannot gain insights. Since Buddhas have attained enlightenment for our sake, why should they abandon us now? Our spiritual teachers are the conduit through which we receive their teachings.

They are kinder to us than even the Buddhas, for though many enlightened beings and Bodhisattvas have come to this world, we were never in the right place at the right time to receive their teachings or to be taken care of by them. Our spiritual teachers appear as ordinary people to whom we can relate. What they do for us is no different from that which an enlightened being would do. If we were to meet Buddhas and Bodhisattvas in person, they would give us the very same teachings.

We read in the stories of the Buddha's past lives that he made enormous sacrifices time and time again for just a few lines of teaching. When we contemplate the lives of teachers, such as Atisha, Marpa and Milarepa, we see what hardships they faced to obtain teachings. Through the kindness of our spiritual teachers we can receive even the exalted teachings of the Great Vehicle in comfort. They pass on these teachings to us in their entirety without any errors, holding nothing back and instructing us clearly, informally and with an open heart, like parents who lovingly advise their children. If we practiced what we have learned from them, we would certainly attain liberation and enlightenment.

When as a result of their kindness we begin to recognize for ourselves what is constructive and what is harmful and act accordingly, transformation takes place. This is a sign that we have received their blessings and that they are taking effect. In times of crisis, the teachings they have given us act as a support and a source of counsel and comfort. In the long run too our accomplishment of common and supreme powerful attainments depends on our teachers' blessings.

Cultivating the relationship with them through our actions consists of pleasing them by what we do. The least way of doing this is by making material gifts. Better than this is to offer them our services and help them in whatever ways are appropriate. This may include nursing them, cooking or fetching and carrying for them or massaging them when they feel stiff or tired. Sakyapandita once asked his uncle Sakya Jetsün Trakpa Gyeltsen[21] how to cultivate the relationship with one's spiritual teacher, but Jetsün Trakpa Gyeltsen replied, "I cannot give you those instructions because you see me just as your uncle and not as an enlightened being." Later Jetsün Trakpa Gyeltsen fell seriously ill and Sakyapandita nursed him day and night with great care and devotion. This caused many inner obstacles to fall away so that he was able to see his spiritual teacher as an enlightened being and when Trakpa Gyeltsen had recovered, he conferred on Sakyapandita the instructions he had requested. Sakyapandita became very learned in the five fields of knowledge and many in positions of authority and influence in Tibet, China and Mongolia placed him on the crown of their heads by regarding him as their spiritual teacher.

By far the finest way to serve our teachers through our actions is by practising the teachings they have given us. By doing this we please them and offer them the only gift they really desire.

GATEWAY FOR THE FORTUNATE

After paying homage, Tsongkhapa makes the commitment to give instruction:

1

**I shall explain as well as I can
The essence of the Victorious Ones' teachings,
The path praised by their excellent children,
The gateway for the fortunate seeking liberation.**

The essence of the Victorious Ones' teachings are the practices associated with the three levels of capacity. These include all the insights one needs in order to gain liberation and enlightenment and are, in turn, included within the three principal paths of insight. These three form a path of spiritual development praised by Buddhas and Bodhisattvas and are the gateway to liberation.

All the teachings given by enlightened ones are intended to help us avoid bad rebirths as well as the many other kinds of suffering associated with cyclic existence and to provide us with the means to reach liberation and enlightenment. For this skillful means and wisdom must be combined. Of the many forms of skillful means, the highest is the altruistic intention to attain enlightenment for the sake of all living beings, and of the many kinds of understanding, the understanding of the fundamental nature of reality is the most profound. A strong wish for freedom from cyclic existence gives us the impetus to develop both of these.

Shantideva reminds us that if we lack compassion and love for ourselves and don't even want to help ourselves, how can we develop the wish to free others, the compassionate wish to alleviate their suffering, the loving wish to give them happiness and the altruistic intention to attain enlightenment for their sake. He says:

> If for your own sake even in your dreams
> This attitude is undreamt of,
> How will it arise for the sake of others?

The three categories of the Buddha's teachings relating to the different kinds of training in ethical discipline, concentration and wisdom, which may also be expressed as training in conduct, meditation and view, can all be condensed into the practices of the three levels of capacity and further abridged, as has been explained, into the three principal paths. When we practice them, we practice everything the Buddha taught.

It isn't possible to drink the milk of a thousand cows in its ordinary form, but we can drink it as condensed milk. We may not be able to eat all the algae that go into a bottle of spirulina or all the young barley plants that make up a jar of barley essence, but the concentrates derived from them are easily absorbed and highly nutritious.

The texts which are known by the generic Tibetan term *lamrim* or "stages of the path" derive this name from Atisha's *Lamp for the Path to Enlightenment*, the teaching he gave when he came to Tibet in response to Lha Lama Jangchup Wö's[22] request for instructions which would benefit not just a select few but everyone. However, texts presenting the stages of the path existed prior to that in India and this style of presentation is intrinsic to the Buddha's teaching. The *Condensed Perfection of Wisdom Sutra*[23] says, "The path of all Victorious Ones of the past, those not yet come and those living now is that of the perfections and no other." These stages of the path are not the invention or prerogative of any particular school or tradition but are relevant to all Buddhist practitioners.

If you want good health, you must insure that your diet is well-balanced and complete. You wouldn't just gobble up anything edible that comes your way. Spiritual food should be approached with equal care. The practices you choose should be genuine and complete. Sakyapandita said that when we're buying a jewel or a horse—and the same would apply these days to buying a car or a house—we shop around and ask others for advice, but a wise or unwise purchase can only affect our fortunes in this life. The spiritual practices we undertake can assure or jeopardize our well-being throughout many future lifetimes and so it is essential to make a wise choice. Milarepa said that unless the teachings we practice are free from errors and have come down to us through a living and uninterrupted tradition, time spent meditating in a mountain retreat will just be self-inflicted misery.

No matter how long you churn water, you will never get any butter, nor will practicing teachings which are incomplete or unauthentic ever yield insights. An authentic teaching has its source in the Buddha's words and has been sufficiently examined by great masters to insure it is free from corruptions and interpolations. Others have gained valid insights through its practice and it has been passed from one living person to another in an unbroken line. The teachings on the stages of the path and on the three principal paths fulfill these criteria.

An alternative interpretation of the verse is that the second, third and fourth lines each refer to one of the principal paths. "The essence of the Victorious Ones' teachings" may then be taken to denote the wish to leave cyclic existence. The Buddha gave teachings which comprise the Hearer Vehicle, the Solitary Realizer Vehicle and the Great Vehicle.[24] Conventionally these appear to lead to different results, but in fact everything the Buddha taught was intended eventually to guide us to the practices of the Great Vehicle and thus to complete enlightenment. The ultimate wish for freedom is the wish to be free from both the fears of cyclic existence and from the dangers of solitary peace.

"The path praised by their excellent children" is the quintessential practice of all Bodhisattvas and the fulcrum of the Great Vehicle—the altruistic intention to attain enlightenment for the sake of all living beings. The Buddha praises the altruistic intention in the *Array of Trunks Sutra*, comparing it to the father and to the seed, while wisdom is likened to the mother. Both are indispensable.

"The gateway for the fortunate who seek liberation" is the correct understanding of reality. The sole way to attain liberation is to cut through the ignorance which lies at the root of our cyclic existence. Only the understanding of selflessness can do this and thus there is no other door to peace.

In these three lines Tsongkhapa summarizes the nature of the three principal insights. The wish for freedom from cyclic existence is fundamental. In *Yogic Deeds of Bodhisattvas* Aryadeva says:

> How can anyone who has no aversion
> To this take an interest in pacification?
> Like leaving home, it is also hard
> To leave worldly existence behind.

Recognition of your present condition and a distaste for the recurrent suffering you experience provide the impetus. If you are feeling cold, you will do nothing about it until you become uncomfortable. Without any aversion to cyclic existence and what it entails, you won't long for freedom or make the effort to attain it. Freedom will therefore continue to elude you.

From another point of view, "the essence of the Victorious Ones' teachings" can be taken to refer to the correct understanding of reality. All the Buddha's teachings are medicine to relieve the unavoidable miseries of cyclic existence. Every part of his teachings has a curative effect on one or another of our ailments.

The *Heart Sutra*, which is the essence of the Perfection of Wisdom sutras,[25] calls the understanding of reality the "mantra of great knowledge." When the two syllables of the Sanskrit word *mantra* are separated, *man* means "mind" and *tra* means "protection." A mantra is therefore something which protects the mind. Insight into the true nature of reality protects us from ignorance and its imprints. Once ignorance is overcome, the disturbing emotions that cause compulsive actions leading to our painful experiences stop.

According to sutra the root of cyclic existence is our misconception that things have true existence. According to tantra this conception and the energy wind on which it rides are responsible. Since mind and energy are always together, tantric practice concentrates on halting the activity of the energy winds which serve as mounts for such conceptions. By gathering these coarser energies into the central channel of the subtle body and by causing them to remain and dissolve there, their activity ceases as does that of the coarser mental states allied to them. This allows subtle awareness to become active. One of the main purposes of tantric practice is to make manifest the actual clear light, namely subtle awareness in a blissful state experiencing reality.

If you wish to take the tantric path to freedom, you need a sound understanding of reality, a strong intention to attain enlightenment for others' sake and an urgent wish to get out of cyclic existence. This is the bedrock on which the whole edifice of tantric practice stands.

These three principal insights are not just something of value to Buddhists. If we look beyond labels and terminology, we will discover the true meaning of these insights and the function they perform. Then we can see whether they have any relevance to us and our situation and can choose whether or not to invest energy in trying to develop them.

Having introduced the three principal insights, Tsong-khapa now urges us to give what follows our full attention.

2

Unattached to the joys of worldly existence,
Striving to use well their freedom and riches,
Trusting the path that pleases the Victors—
Fortunate ones, listen with a pure mind.

Who are the fortunate? The Buddha's precious teachings are for us and we are entitled to our share of them. If you were invited to a sumptuous dinner and everyone but you was served, you would feel upset, but nothing more than a few hours with an empty stomach would be at stake. Does it disturb you to think you might miss your share of the Buddha's teachings? Would you feel deprived and consider it the loss of something valuable?

The truly fortunate are those indifferent even to the most enthralling pleasures of cyclic existence. Recognizing the rarity and value of a human life in which they enjoy many freedoms and riches, they are as single-minded about attaining liberation as someone whose hair has caught fire would be about extinguishing it. They feel a strong conviction regarding the path to enlightenment, the path which the Victorious Ones delight to see us follow. Do we meet these criteria? What does indifference to the delights of cyclic existence mean? We need neither destroy our pleasure in them nor ignore them but must overcome our addictive craving for them.

This may seem light-years away from your present condition, but consider, for instance, that skilled artisans don't start out that way. Natural talent is essential, but they also have to learn and practice the many techniques of their craft. If you have the right inclination, you can develop the characteristics of a fine practitioner as described by Tsongkhapa.

The teachings are the medicine we need to alleviate our suffering. They heal us, assuage our spiritual hunger and thirst, and nourish us. Human beings have the exceptional potential to gain lasting happiness and rid themselves completely of suffering. The teachings equip us to do this. Tsongkhapa encourages us to approach the teachings with a pure mind—free from the faults which make us like a pot that is upside down, a pot with a hole or a dirty pot—and with the six attitudes already explained.

1 THE WISH FOR FREEDOM

THE FETTERS

The text now examines the reasons for developing the wish to leave cyclic existence and how the wish is aroused. It also defines what it means to have developed that wish.

3

**Without the wish for freedom there is no way to calm
The pursuit of pleasant effects in the sea of worldly existence.
Since those with bodies are fettered by their thirst for being,
First seek the wish to leave cyclic existence.**

Without this wish you remain preoccupied only with the glories of cyclic existence and lack the incentive to free yourself. A prisoner serving a life-sentence, who feels comfortable in jail, makes no attempt to escape and so will never be free. If our wish to find a way out of cyclic existence is sufficiently strong, we will definitely reach freedom.

As long as we have a contaminated body and mind[1] which result from actions underlain by the disturbing emotions, we are in cyclic existence. Disturbing emotions stimulate compulsive actions, giving rise to rebirth with a contaminated body and mind. Ignorance causes craving, which provokes action and leads to further rebirth of the same kind. And so the process continues interminably life after life.

The fetters of contaminated action and disturbing emotions keep us bound to this cycle of involuntary birth and death. What is bound? Our mental consciousness which continues from one life to the next. At present we lack control over our destiny because we are driven by these emotions, whose dictates we obey. Such a total lack of freedom, in which we are governed by other forces that do nothing but harm us, is clearly a condition of suffering. Cyclic existence is synonymous with suffering. Only when we recognize this and feel an intense antipathy for it will the wish to extricate ourselves arise.

People who are rich and influential experience much anxiety about gaining and retaining wealth and authority. They are consumed by fear of losing what they possess. Though, of course, they too experience physical pain, their suffering is chiefly mental. Those who are poor and without influence experience constant physical hardship as they try to find the basic necessities of life—food, clothing and shelter. In rich countries we forget that these are the main concerns of most people in the world, who are simply struggling to survive. Their suffering is mainly physical, though naturally they also experience anxiety. Everyone faces trouble and sorrow.

Without a strong drive to free yourself from cyclic existence you will continue to desire the pleasures of this world. You may think, "Well, what's wrong with that?" The quest to find happiness in these ordinary pleasures keeps you bound to worldly existence and the satisfaction you seek will always elude you. Though craving itself is different from the basic misconception of the self which lies at the root of our suffering, this thirst experienced by beings with bodies keeps us chained to suffering in every way. If you are carrying the wood of a prickly thorn-tree on your naked back, no matter which way you turn or shift the load, you will never find a moment's comfort until you set it down.

In our heart of hearts we know that our present condition is uncomfortable. Wherever we travel we are reminded of it because sooner or later something goes wrong—either we get sick or unhappy. No matter how great the luxury we enjoy or the excellent company we keep, misery of some kind dogs our footsteps.

Cyclic existence is not a place. Places are easy enough to leave. Nor does cyclic existence only affect certain species or groups of people. It affects every ordinary living being. Our lack of understanding is the root of our suffering and is responsible for our troubles. The emphasis placed on education is a sign that this is generally recognized, but the knowledge most educational institutions impart is relevant only to the concerns of this life and therefore cannot help to free us. The second most invidious factor that fetters us is craving. In the twelve-part process through which we remain within cyclic existence,[2] ignorance, craving and grasping prepare the ground for suffering.

Ignorance is our confusion regarding the fundamental nature of things, particularly of the self. Without it the strong sense of "I" does not arise. Though there is a self, our ignorance magnifies it disproportionately, causing intense disturbing emotions to arise. Focusing on this false self, we are preoccupied with its happiness. Craving is the desire for that happiness, while grasping reaches out for it. These two must be stopped if we are to gain nirvana.

How is it done? First create a good motivation to do what is constructive and turn your mind towards the teachings. Work at decreasing your desires and cultivating contentment. Just this alone would increase your happiness dramatically, whereas the insatiable desire for better friends, lovers and possessions creates a continual and depressing sense of poverty.

A multitude of disturbing emotions and carelessness are responsible for our unwholesome physical actions and speech. Ethical discipline consists of decreasing such actions and the craving to have the best of everything just for ourselves. While these concerns haunt us, our practice will not be genuine, even if we meditate intensively day and night. Pure practice can arise only when we stop craving the ordinary pleasures of this life as well as the joys and comforts of future lives.

Developing the wish to leave cyclic existence encompasses the practices of the initial and intermediate levels of the path. You might think that since you want to attain Buddhahood, you could just devote your efforts to developing the altruistic intention and that there is no need to arouse a wish to leave cyclic existence, since you have vowed to take rebirth in cyclic existence again and again for the sake of others. However, only a very strong personal wish to escape from cyclic existence will make you aspire to gain enlightenment. Unless you fully recognize your own condition of suffering and want to free yourself, you will never feel the intense compassion for others in a similar condition, which eventually gives birth to the altruistic intention.

The Kadampa master Geshe Sharawa[3] used a homely example: if we don't have a real desire to rid ourselves of the disturbing emotions and actions that keep us trapped in this cycle of birth and death—a desire which results from seeing their faults—our wish to leave cyclic existence and our aspiration for freedom will be merely superficial. If you sprinkle tsampa—parched barley flour, the Tibetan staple—on beer, it just floats on the surface.

Just understanding what the wish to leave cyclic existence and the altruistic intention entail does not make you a real practitioner. These attitudes must be so deeply ingrained that they become the motivating force for everything you do.

THIRST FOR PLEASURE

The way to make your practice pure and to develop the wish to escape from the cycle of involuntary birth and death is first to overcome longing directed towards the things of this life.

4

Freedom and riches are hard to find; life is fleeting—
Familiarity with this stops clinging to this life's pleasures.
Repeatedly considering actions, their unfailing effects
As well as the suffering of cyclic existence
Stops clinging to future pleasures.

Thinking about the preciousness of your human condition and its transient nature helps you to do this.

In his quintessential instructions for training the mind called *Parting from the Four Attachments*[4] the great Sakya Jetsün Trakpa Gyeltsen said, "If you are attached to this life, you are no practitioner. If you are attached to cyclic existence, you have no wish to leave it." Whether you are a true practitioner is determined by whether or not you have let go of worldly matters. Worldly concerns and seemingly spiritual activities, such as reciting prayers, can go hand in hand, but authentic practice will never mesh with worldly ways.

Real practice depends on your thoughts and intentions. Dromtönpa once saw a monk circumambulating a stupa and addressed him respectfully, "Master, doing circumambulations is good, but it would be better to practice." So the monk decided to try prostrations and was energetically engaged in this, when Dromtönpa said the same thing to him. Next the monk devoted himself to recitation and then to meditation, but each time Dromtönpa made the same remark. Thoroughly perplexed, the monk asked Dromtönpa what he meant by practice. Dromtönpa emphatically repeated "Give up this life!" three times.

Don't misunderstand this to mean you must give away all your possessions and leave your family, your home or your job. It is about overcoming attachment. A Tibetan master, Shang Nachung Tönpa,[5] again and again requested Atisha to teach him, but Atisha only told him, "Let go! Cultivate love, compassion and the altruistic intention." Nachung Tönpa

complained that this was all Atisha had said. When
Dromtönpa heard of his complaint, he commented, "Doesn't
he realize that he's received the pith of our lord Atisha's instructions? Even someone as great as Shang doesn't know what
it is to receive a teaching." Eventually Nachung Tönpa took to
heart what Atisha had told him and began giving his students
the same advice: let go of attachment and be kind-hearted.

Concern for this life mars what we do and prevents practices
from being authentic, while even quite an ordinary action done
with the wish to escape from cyclic existence becomes a valid
practice of the Buddha's teaching. Love, compassion and the
intention to become enlightened for others' sake makes that same
action a Mahayana practice. Otherwise no matter what elabo-
rate rituals we perform, they are merely like the tsampa floating
on the beer.

Letting go of our preoccupation with the things of this life
involves giving up the eight worldly concerns, which in short
depends on overcoming attachment to food, clothing and
reputation. Many meditators, scholars and monks happily
forego good food and clothing, and live a simple life, yet they
remain attached to a good reputation, which is hardest to
give up. Above the entrance to the cave it may say, "Retreat
in progress. Do not disturb," but inside the retreatant is hoping for recognition as a great meditator. The scholar has hopes
of acclaim for his great knowledge and the monk for his pure
morality. Such thoughts attract obstacles and prevent anything
valuable from being accomplished. If letting go of our attachments is the door to pure practice, we must look within and
see where we stand. It is not easy to be a true practitioner.

In his *Letter to a Friend*, Nagarjuna[6] says:

> Worldly wise one, the eight worldly concerns
> Are getting and not getting, happiness and unhappiness,
> Fame and disrepute, praise and blame. Without letting them
> Be objects of your mind, treat them as the same.

As long as you are pleased to receive gifts and rewards, to
be happy, well thought of or praised and are displeased

when you do not receive rewards and material gain, when you are unhappy, ill thought of or criticized, these considerations will influence your feelings and actions, and no matter how carefully or intensively you perform formal practices, they will be of no real benefit. It is essential to stop the habit of thinking, "If only I could have this, everything would be fine."

The great master Lingrepa[7] reiterates this:

> In this city of preconceptions, cyclic existence,
> The zombies of the eight worldly concerns scurry.
> Here there is a fearsome burial ground! Master, if you wish
> To make things the same taste, do it towards this.

Yang Gönpa, student of the great master Götsangpa[8] says, "It's no use if the teachings are on the Great Completion,[9] unless the person measures up to the Great Completion. Many speak of practices worth a horse, but I see a lot of people worth less than a dog. When the teachings become mere words and are not put into practice, they're no different from what a parrot recites. If your mind and the teachings are like tsampa and water that haven't been mixed and there's a gap between the teachings and your mind big enough for a man to pass through, if the teachings are just floating around on top, like lung when it's cooking, the purpose of the teachings has definitely not been accomplished. As for me, I've made letting go of this life the heart of my practice. Take heed everyone!"

It is one thing to dispute the value of the Buddha's teaching and have no belief in it, but quite another if one claims to follow the Buddha and studies his teachings yet doesn't practice or take them to heart. Parrots can be taught to recite, monkeys can learn to make prostrations and you can teach a dog to beg, which makes it look as if it's praying. To avoid merely aping practice, listen and study the teachings well. Think about what you have learned until you gain a proper understanding and then familiarize yourself with it until it begins to influence how you think and feel. This will affect how you act and speak. When your physical, verbal and mental actions begin to accord with the Buddha's teachings, you will experience happiness and become a trustworthy example to others.

The Kadampa masters advised us to cultivate ten jewel-like attitudes. The first four of these attitudes concern four kinds of entrustment. The first is the innermost attitude of entrusting yourself completely to the teachings. To develop this attitude, consider the preciousness of your human life, the rarity of a life like this and how meaningful it is in terms of your potential. How brief life is! You have no idea when you will die. It can happen at any moment and at that time neither your possessions, friends nor even your body can help or save you. Nothing but the teachings is of any use then.

Seen from that perspective, accumulating wealth and property and trying to surround yourself with the right friends or supporters is quite meaningless, since you can take none of these with you when you go. In trying to fulfill such desires, you perform many misdeeds whose consequences must be experienced in the future. You entrust yourself to the teachings by putting them at the heart of everything you think and do, by constantly trying to be positive and kind-hearted and by expressing this in action.

The second of these jewel-like attitudes is to entrust yourself to poverty in your practice of the teachings. You do not need to live a life of poverty, but if necessary you should be ready to do so by overcoming attachment to pleasurable sights, sounds, smells, tastes and tactile sensations. This will bring you contentment. How can you hope to reconcile an unquenchable thirst for the best of these things, which consumes your attention and energy, with true practice?

Perhaps you fear that by putting the teachings at the center of your life, you will one day lack even the most basic amenities and become so poor that you will be forced to beg. But if you entrust yourself to poverty and summon up courage to devote all your energy to practicing the teachings come what may, paradoxically you will never lack what you need. The Buddha himself predicted that those of his followers who practiced with dedication would never die of starvation. There is a saying that if the meditator doesn't roll down the mountain, the food will roll up.

Before the Kadampa master Geshe Bengungyel[10] reformed, he owned so many fields in Pempo[11] that forty bags of barley seed were needed at sowing time. He robbed by day and thieved by night but never had enough to eat, yet when he began to practice the Buddha's teachings, he had more than enough. He said, "Before my mouth couldn't find food, but now the food can't find my mouth."

Pempo, where many of the Kadampa masters lived, has good fertile land. It was a custom in my part of Kham for the young women to go on pilgrimage before they got married. A group of them would secretly arrange to travel together and in the third or fourth Tibetan month[12] they would slip away from home and set out on foot for central Tibet. They did not mind leaving the comforts of home behind to go on this adventure. They carried only a small pack and a big stick to keep off the dogs that guarded the houses where they begged for food and shelter along the way. Dogs in Tibet were big and fierce and it was their job to bite intruders, but two young women standing back to back with their sturdy sticks could fend off even the fiercest dog.

They reached Pempo in the sixth or seventh month and looked for work on the farms. When the harvest had been brought in, they were paid in barley. They then made their way to Lhasa where they sold half the barley and used the other half for tsampa. With this money and food they set out on pilgrimage for three months, visiting temples, monasteries and sacred places.

They returned to Lhasa just before the Tibetan New Year. Quite a few traders and merchants from my area of Kham lived in Lhasa. The young women would borrow good clothes from them and perform our local songs and dances, which these people living far from home thoroughly enjoyed. They would give the young women money with which to buy presents and a few useful things from the city before they began their long journey back to Kham.

This was the first independent action these young women had ever undertaken in their lives and though they left secretly, they had their parents' tacit permission because it was a long-standing custom. They returned proud of the pilgrimage they had made and happy to have visited the statue of the Buddha in the main temple in Lhasa, revered throughout Tibet as the "Wish-fulfilling Lord."[13]

You may worry about the possibility that if you put nothing away for a rainy day and are reduced to penury, you might even die of starvation. Reflect on the fact that you have died countless times in the past but never once for the sake of the teachings. Everyone, whether rich or poor, must die eventually, so even if you were to die, this time it would be for a worthwhile reason. People create many harmful actions for the sake of wealth and it is better to die poor without having done such things. The third jewel-like attitude is to entrust yourself even to death from hunger or cold with the resolve never to stop practicing.

Now you might be anxious about who will look after you when you grow old and who will dispose of your body in the proper way when you die. Such worries reveal that you are still ensnared by worldly concerns. You may live to be old, but it is not at all certain. Shantideva says:

> Go to the cremation ground and think
> Those others' bones and my body
> Both have the nature to disintegrate
> And so one day they will be alike.

He tells us to go and look at the bleached bones lying there. Once they were part of others' bodies, cherished as we now cherish our own body, but those people had to part from their bodies which decayed and lacked independent existence. Our bodies are no different and one day the same thing will happen to us. Courageously entrust yourself to an empty cave, thinking even if for the sake of your practice you have to die alone like a dog far away from everyone in a desolate place, you will not be afraid or distressed. This is the fourth jewel-like attitude.

The Buddha's life teaches us about the four attitudes of entrustment. Leaving behind the luxury of his father's palace he adopted the simple life of an itinerant ascetic and devoted himself wholly to practice. He lived as a mendicant with no fear of poverty and undertook extremely austere practices for six years by the river Nairanjana, ready even to face death in a desolate place far from any habitation. This shows us the importance of complete trust and dedication.

When monks or nuns become ordained, they promise to make some radical changes: to leave behind family life and all signs of a secular life-style and to adopt the marks of an ordained person. They receive a religious name to remind them of this. During the ordination ceremony they are told that from then on they should live on alms, wear robes made of patched cloth and make do with ordinary or left-over medicines when they are sick, instead of seeking expensive remedies and treatments. This denotes their willingness to die if necessary. They are to seek shelter under trees and in disused and ruined buildings. These precepts delineate an ideal of simplicity, but of course only a few practitioners have the stamina to adopt such a way of life.

Milarepa says:

> Without loved ones to know of my happiness,
> Nor enemies to know of my suffering,
> If I could die in this mountain retreat
>   A yogi's wish would be fulfilled.

> Without friends to know I'm growing old,
> Nor my sister to know when I am sick,
> If I could die in this mountain retreat
>   A yogi's wish would be fulfilled.

> Without people knowing when I am dead,
> My rotting body unseen by birds,
> If I could die in this mountain retreat
>   A yogi's wish would be fulfilled.

Just flies to suck my flesh and bones
And worms to eat my veins and sinews,
If I could die in this mountain retreat
    A yogi's wish would be fulfilled.

No human traces at my door,
And inside no trace of blood,
If I could die in this mountain retreat
    A yogi's wish would be fulfilled.

Without any people around my corpse,
And none to weep when I'm dead,
If I could die in this mountain retreat
    A yogi's wish would be fulfilled.

With none to ask where I have gone,
And no certainty that "He went there,"
If I could die in this mountain retreat
    A yogi's wish would be fulfilled.

May this beggar's last prayer at death
Made in a cave in a desolate place
Be for the good of living beings,
    And if it be, my wish is fulfilled.

Such utter dedication to practice of the teachings is the road many great masters of India and Tibet have taken. Follow in their footsteps and avoid the by-ways on which it is easy to get lost. A friend was driving in Australia and decided to take a short cut. She told me, "This is the vajra path," but she soon discovered that she had taken a wrong turn!

Three adamantine resolutions follow the four kinds of entrustment in the list of the ten jewel-like attitudes held dear by the Kadampa masters. The first consists of being immutably invulnerable to objections. Your parents and other loved ones will worry over what might happen to you if you give up all normal concerns and devote yourself entirely to the teachings. "How will you manage?" they'll say tearfully, and you will feel guilty at causing them so much sadness and anxiety. Let nothing they say deflect you from your purpose, and hold firmly to your resolution.

The Buddha left his parents, his wives and his companions at court to live in a way that he hoped would ultimately make him of greater use to them. Atisha too gave up a royal life, and although his father could not bear the prospect of separation, Atisha reassured him that by enduring this parting they would never be separated in future lives.

The second adamantine resolution is to maintain an immutable lack of embarrassment. When you adopt such an unconventional life-style, others may deride you and say that you are no better than a beggar. Whether they call you a god or a devil, remain resolutely unembarrassed and untouched by their derision. Trying to live in accordance with your relations' wishes is frequently a hindrance to pure practice. You can reject their values without rejecting them or giving up your love and compassion for them. The Buddha's secret departure from the royal palace, which caused his father grief, was not motivated by a lack of filial affection but by his wish to gain spiritual insights.

The third adamantine resolution is to consort with immutable wisdom. Having committed yourself to certain practices, be steadfast and never transgress the promises you have made. Let go of everything that could tempt you to do so and devote yourself entirely and single-mindedly to the accomplishment of your aims. For six years the Buddha did not waver from his practice of the meditative stabilization known as "Pervading Space."[14] This meditation focuses on the fundamental nature of phenomena, which is present wherever there is space. Everywhere throughout space there are suffering living beings on whom this meditation also focuses with the compassionate wish to relieve their suffering and the loving wish to give them happiness. Thus it combines essential wisdom and skillful means.

There will be three results from behaving in a way which seems to show an outrageous disregard for conventional values. You place yourself outside the accepted norms of society, and others, whatever their social standing, will consider you insane because you are uninterested in the very things they consider of overriding importance and to which they devote their time and energy. They will shun you because they consider your conduct a challenge to their way of life and so you will find yourself expelled from human society.

The Buddha left the society of the court in which he had lived and set out alone to wander in uninhabited places. Great masters like Atisha, Shantideva and others also had the courage to leave the comforts of a royal life behind. If we claim to be their followers, even though we may not ourselves be able to emulate their example, we can at least admire their actions and consider their implications.

On the fringes of society as a homeless outcast, you will find yourself in the company of dogs. Like a stray dog you will have to bear whatever hardships you face in obtaining food and shelter without complaint and without allowing it to shake your decision to practice. When the Buddha sat meditating on the banks of Nairanjana, he looked so emaciated that even the cowherds who occasionally passed that way mocked him, but nothing could deter him.

As a result of such resolute practice you will attain the divine state of enlightenment, just as the Buddha did, which made him an object of homage by gods and humans. These are the "jewels" of the Kadampa tradition.[15] Contemplating them will enrich you and make you courageous. They express a complete turning away from all worldly concerns. If you adopt them, you will become fearless and your wishes will be fulfilled.

Many great and admired practitioners did not embrace a life of poverty or give away all their possessions, yet they practiced purely because they relinquished worldly concerns. Gaining true insight into the preciousness of your human life and its transient nature makes your practice so pure that you feel no craving, even if every luxury imaginable could be yours. Worldly wealth and status will have as little appeal to you as a plateful of the food that has just turned your stomach.

Though a certain degree of understanding can arise from listening to the teachings, insights will only be stable if they result from deep personal reflection and experience. The difference is like driving a dagger into mud, where it won't remain firm, and driving it into solid earth. Your insights must enter and become deeply embedded in your heart.

LIFE IS FLEETING

Tsongkhapa says, "Freedom and riches are hard to find and life is fleeting." Freedom refers to being free from hindrances which would prevent us from engaging in spiritual practice. The riches we enjoy are many external and internal conditions conducive to our practice of the teachings. Such a life is meaningful because we can accomplish anything on which we set our hearts. Particularly we can insure our well-being in future lives and even attain highest enlightenment because we possess every potential necessary for this.

A privileged life of this kind is indeed hard to find and demands the creation of very special causes of which the principal is ethical discipline. Only we can judge whether our way of life is truly ethical. A human life is also seen to be rare when we consider that there are many more living beings in bad rebirths than there are in good ones and far fewer humans than other kinds of creatures. Among humans how rare it is to enjoy the leisure and fortune we have!

In a big city we are surrounded by people, but how many enjoy the freedoms and riches which make this life precious in terms of spiritual practice? How many of them have any interest whatsoever in such matters? Only when we fully recognize the value of our life do we understand that every day and every moment can be meaningful. What do we value more, our human life and potential or our material possessions?

Once we are aware of life's value, we must decide on the best way to use it. The choices we make will have lasting implications. A good and safe beginning is to learn how to combine kindness with intelligence. We acquire skills or knowledge in order to apply them and if our intention is good, some benefit will result from using what our intelligence has enabled us to learn. If our motivation is mediocre, the result will be no better, and if we have a dishonest or harmful intention, it is likely that we will make bad use of our knowledge. Kindness is essential, since excellence in a particular field is no guarantee that one will not misuse one's expertise. For instance, a very extensive knowledge of the Buddha's teachings can be used for anything, such as self-aggrandizement or personal profit. Our quintessential purpose should always remain the attainment of enlightenment for others' sake.

To remind us of the rarity of a human life like ours, Shantideva used the following analogy:

> Therefore the Conqueror said that just like
> A turtle putting its neck through the hole
> Of a yoke floating on a vast ocean,
> A human life is extremely hard to find.

A blind turtle lives on the ocean bed and surfaces just once every hundred years. A golden yoke floats on the vast ocean, blown here and there by the wind. What are the chances of the turtle surfacing at just the right time and in just the right place to be able to put its head through the yoke? Our chances of gaining a life of freedom and fortune are just as improbable. You may think it couldn't possibly be so difficult, but cyclic existence is like a vast and stormy ocean and we are like the turtle that spends most of its time in the depths and only surfaces very occasionally. For most of our lives we have been in bad rebirths and it happens only very rarely that we emerge from these into a good rebirth.

The yoke is made of gold and is therefore heavy, so it often sinks and is invisible. The yoke symbolizes the teachings of an enlightened one. An age of illumination is a period during which an enlightened one has taught in the world and those teachings are still extant, but there are much longer dark periods of time when the world is without such teachings.

The yoke does not remain in one place but is blown here and there by the wind. Similarly the teachings first flourish in one country and then in another. They thrive where people take an interest in practicing them and die out when they cease to be alive in people's hearts. Sometimes the turtle comes up to the surface but in a place where there is no golden yoke. This is like taking a good rebirth but having no access to the teachings.

The turtle must actually put its head into the yoke, which signifies that the only way into the teachings is by taking refuge in the Three Jewels. Our lack of interest in the teachings and our reluctance to engage with them is due to our lack of intelligence, which is like the turtle's blindness. No matter what good circumstances we enjoy, our life is not truly fortunate and free from obstacles if we have no interest in the Buddha's teachings.

Don't treat the story of the turtle merely as an amusing little fable, but allow it to act as a vivid reminder of how rare your present situation is. There are many good uses to which you can put your human life and when you are conscious of its true value, you will surely wish to choose the very best. What could be better than developing the wish to leave cyclic existence, the altruistic intention to attain enlightenment for the sake of others and the correct understanding of reality?

Despite what most of us see daily on our television screens or hear on the radio, we fail to realize how rare it is to enjoy a life of so much freedom, fortune and opportunity. How long can we expect to live? We may die at sixty, or perhaps we will live to be seventy or eighty. A few people even live to be a hundred. How much of our life is gone and what have we done with it so far? Unless we have clairvoyant powers, we cannot predict when death will come. We may have another twenty, thirty or forty years left. If we are young, we may feel that most of our life is yet to come, but what if we are destined to have a short life?

If we cannot point to anything we have done which has been genuinely constructive for ourselves and others, then from the point of view of the Buddha's teachings we have wasted our time. And unless we make some changes now, we will probably remain the slaves of our food, clothing, property and reputations for the rest of our lives. While these engross us, time passes and life will soon be over. No matter how long we live, we will never find time to practice.

In his *Letter to a Friend* Nagarjuna says:

> Many things threaten life, which is even more
> Ephemeral than a bubble of water full of air.
> How amazing is the opportunity to exhale
> After inhaling and to awake from sleep.

So little can be relied upon to sustain life but many things can turn into causes of death. Our life is as vulnerable and ephemeral as a bubble. When you went to bed last night, you took it for granted that you would wake up this morning, but how could you be sure? Since death is always just a breath away, it is amazing and wonderful that you are still alive to-day. Many great masters in Tibet were so conscious of death's imminence that they would turn the wooden bowl from which they ate and drank upside down before they went to bed, indicating by this gesture that perhaps there would be no further use for the bowl next day. Many apparently healthy people die in their sleep. You must have heard of such cases.

Meditation on impermanence and the imminence of death is certainly not a cheerful topic and may have a very depress-ing effect. All of us, except small children, know that since we have been born, we will certainly die. But merely think-ing about the incontestable fact that we will die is not what is known as meditation on death and impermanence. Instead think about the fact that from the moment you were conceived in your mother's womb, you began dying and remember that there isn't much time left. In *Yogic Deeds of Bodhisattvas* Aryadeva says:

> Those who are born only to die
> And whose nature is to be driven
> Appear to be in the act of dying
> And not in the act of living.

Life itself seems to be in death's service, since every moment of life brings us closer to death. Death's minions, sickness, ageing and decline, lead us to the slaughter. In the stories of the Buddha Shakyamuni's past lives it says:

> Heroic ruler, from that first night
> Of entering an earthly womb from elsewhere,
> Starting then and day by day
> One approaches death unceasingly.

Whether you are walking, sitting, standing or lying down, every moment takes you nearer to death, when nothing you normally rely on, such as your possessions, loved ones or even your body, can help you. The messenger of a despotic and merciless king who has sent him on a mission and threatened him with execution if he does not return at the appointed time keeps on the move and never rests for a moment. Similarly life never stops for an instant but keeps going and relentlessly carries out death's mission.

A female ascetic wanted to enter her home but a camel was lying outside her door. As she stepped over it, the camel jumped up in fright and bolted with her on its back. Just as she was powerless to direct it but had to go where it took her, once we are born, ageing and sickness carry us willy-nilly towards death. We are utterly in death's power.

If a hired assassin fails to kill his victim, he will kill the person who hired him instead. What has been born cannot remain alive and instead performs the function of dying. Contemplation of the meaning of these unusual analogies, found in Chandrakirti's commentary[16] on Aryadeva's *Yogic Deeds of Bodhisattvas*, can have a powerful effect in diminishing our preoccupation with the well-being of this life.

Just knowing that you must die will not change you, but reflecting deeply and continually on death's proximity will. Now is the time to begin practicing, before it is too late—not tomorrow nor at some unspecified date in the future—because death can come at any moment. If you don't remember death you will not think of practicing, since you will be too wrapped up in your ordinary activities. Even if you do think about spiritual practice, unless you remember death, you won't actually do anything but will keep delaying. You may eventually begin to practice, but if you don't remember death, you will not practice purely and may well use practice as a way to accomplish your worldly aims. Even if you practice with a good motivation, your practice will lack intensity and your approach will be casual unless you remember death.

At present the impact the teachings have made on us is as superficial and transient as a drawing on water, while our bad habits and disturbing emotions are as deeply incised as an engraving in stone. We must reverse this by insuring that our disturbing emotions and negative actions are short-lived and that the impression left by the teachings is lasting.

If you fail to remember death, you will make numerous plans for this life. To accomplish them you will need many things and your desires will never allow you to be content. Looking after your friends and loved ones and opposing those you dislike will preoccupy you. Instead of becoming more pliant, like green wood, your mind will grow more and more stubborn and unbending, like a stiff dry stick. Your harmful actions, lost opportunities and the time you have wasted will cause you much regret when death comes. Remembering death, on the other hand, is beneficial and meaningful. The realization that you could die at any time makes you more generous and ethical, which has a profound effect on your future.

The most powerful insight of all is the understanding of emptiness because of its capacity to uproot ignorance, but recollecting the imminence of death is certainly a close second, since it simultaneously deals a crushing blow both to our harmful behavior and to the emotional habits which cause it. At the outset remembering death makes us start to practice. Intermediately it forces us to continue and finally it insures that we bring our practices to completion.

The first time the Buddha taught after his enlightenment he explained the four noble truths. He began by speaking about impermanence in the context of the truth of suffering. At the end of his life he also spoke of impermanence. Remembering the transience of our human life helps us to practice purely. The best kind of practitioner dies with joy. A mediocre practitioner has no fears and the least accomplished practitioner has no regrets.

In his *Great Exposition of the Stages of the Path* Tsongkhapa explains how to meditate on death by means of three roots, nine reasons and three decisions. First think about the fact that death is certain. When death actually comes, nothing you do can avert it. Bribery, flattery and physical strength, which are often used to get one out of awkward situations, are all to no avail. Your life-span, which is determined by your past actions, is like the finite amount of water in a tank. Imagine that the inlet is blocked to prevent any more water from entering and that the outlet is open and the water is running out. Nothing will be added to it. The time you have left to live is constantly dwindling.

Half of our life is spent sleeping and the other half is spent shopping, cooking, eating, drinking and talking. Even a good practitioner, never mind the rest of us, only manages five or six years of concentrated practice in a lifetime. How much of each day do we devote to practice even under the best conditions? Thinking about this stops equivocation as to whether or not to practice and creates a sense of urgency.

Though you know that you must die, remember that whether you are old or young, there is absolutely no certainty as to when death will come. Human beings do not have a fixed life-span and while many things can cause death, few can be relied upon to sustain life. The newspapers tell us daily that the very things intended to prolong life and make it more comfortable can turn into death traps. Life is as tenuous as a flame in the wind and though you may feel strong, your human body is in fact frail and vulnerable. The mutation of a tiny cell is enough to precipitate death. Reflecting on this will stop you from putting off practice until tomorrow and make you decide to start at once.

When death comes, nothing but your practice of the teachings is of any use. Neither your property, loved ones nor even your own body can help you at that time. In fact your attachment to these may prove disastrous in terms of your rebirth. Remembering this helps you to make the decision to do nothing but practice.

Those who do not understand the purpose of meditating on the imminence of death are simply pained and filled with horror at the thought of parting with everything they love. Indeed, if you are not prepared for death, the process of separation will be painful. As a result of this meditation, intelligent people realize the pressing need to purify negative actions and create positive energy before death comes. If they have done this they can die without fear or regret.

ACTIONS AND THEIR CONSEQUENCES

Tsongkhapa speaks of overcoming our clinging to future pleasures with the words, "Repeatedly considering actions, their unfailing effects as well as the suffering of cyclic existence stops clinging to future pleasures." The expression "future pleasures"[17] refers to the excellent physical form, possessions, places and companions we may hope to enjoy in future rebirths as humans or celestial beings. These pleasures may also be taken to include everything associated with a pure land,[18] when our wish to be born there is not out of altruistic concern for others but out of a wish for security and personal freedom from suffering. Doing practices which lead to rebirth in a pure land is desirable when they are done not out of self-interest but with an altruistic intention, since in such an environment conditions most favorable to speed us towards enlightenment prevail. Although the desire for wellbeing in future rebirths is neither harmful nor in conflict with sincere practice of the teachings, it is a hindrance if one is seeking freedom from cyclic existence.

In *The Great Exposition of the Stages of the Path* Tsongkhapa shows that the practices of the initial level are aimed at overcoming attachment to the pleasures of this life. These practices consist of recognizing the preciousness and transience of our human life, thinking about the suffering experienced in bad states of rebirth, taking refuge and reflecting on the connection between actions and their effects. The practices of the intermediate level are intended to overcome clinging to the pleasures of future rebirths. Here, in *The Three Principal Aspects of the Path*, Tsongkhapa designates meditation on the preciousness of our human life and on its transience as the practices which destroy our preoccupation with this life. He designates meditation on the connection between actions and their effects and on the suffering experienced in cyclic existence as the means to overcome clinging to the pleasures we hope for in future rebirths.

Until we gain liberation, we will continue to suffer repeated involuntary birth and death as a result of our actions. To attain liberation we must rid ourselves completely of all activity, wholesome or unwholesome, that is underlain by ignorance, since this keeps us tied to cyclic existence.

The only way to liberation is by putting the teachings into practice and this cannot be done unless we take into consideration the subtle and complex connection between actions and their effects. Obviously this requires a conviction that such a connection exists. Reflecting again and again on actions and their consequences gives rise to this conviction. Contemplation of this kind is a path of practice praised by and pleasing to the Victorious Ones, who are exclusively concerned with our well-being and are happy when we do what will help us.

When thinking about karma—the unfailing connection between actions and their effects—there are four general points which apply to all actions, whether they are positive or negative.[19] The Buddha said that actions and their effects are definite, in the sense that each of the many different actions we perform produces its own specific and individual result, just as barley seed produces barley and wheat seed produces wheat.

He said that actions and their effects grow, for no matter how small an action is, it can produce significant results, just as one small seed can produce the root, trunk, branches, leaves, blossom and fruit of a huge tree. We should not think that a small negative action is nothing to worry about, since it can produce significant consequences and for the same reason even the most insignificant good deed is worth performing.

We have a tendency towards wishful thinking but are reluctant to do what is necessary to make our wishes come true. It is no good hoping to experience the results of virtue which we have not created. If we have not performed an action, we will not experience its result.

An action once performed is not lost. If we have created a negative action, we will have to experience its consequences although we do not want to suffer. The only way to avoid suffering is not to create its causes or to purify the unwholesome actions we have performed. Shantideva says:

> Though you wish to be rid of suffering,
> You run headlong towards suffering.
> Though you desire happiness, your confusion
> Makes you destroy it as you would an enemy.

Conviction regarding the connection between actions and their effects gives us the incentive to adopt what needs to be cultivated and get rid of what must be discarded, which is how the Buddha's teachings are practiced.

In *The Great Exposition of the Stages of the Path* the explanation of the preciousness of our human existence and its transience is followed by a description of suffering in bad states of rebirth and instructions on how to take refuge. This sequence is based on the following contemplation: our precious human life provides us with the freedom and fortune to accomplish enduring happiness, but this life will not last long and we can die at any moment. Death is not like the snuffing out of a candle, since our consciousness will go on to another life. At present we have no control over this process but must take rebirth wherever our past actions propel us.

We have performed all kinds of actions and depending on which imprint is most influential at death, we will take either a good or a bad rebirth. What are our mental and emotional habits? Have we performed more wholesome or unwholesome actions? Only we can make an honest assessment and know the true state of affairs. No one can tell by looking at us. If we are in the habit of thinking and acting constructively, we have created positive energy and our habitual patterns of thought will assert themselves at death, since what is familiar comes to the fore when conscious control weakens. We may look and sound like practitioners, but if our hearts are empty of positive feelings and old negative habits are still firmly entrenched, our prospects are bleak.

A preponderance of negative actions will lead to a rebirth in one of the three bad states. Those in the hells are tormented by intense heat or cold. Hungry spirits constantly experience starvation and thirst, while animals suffer fear and exploitation as a result of their limited intelligence. The suffering of animals is evident everywhere, but in order to imagine the suffering in the other states, think of the worst human suffering of heat, cold, hunger, thirst and terror possible and then magnify it many times.

Could you bear such suffering? Sufficient contemplation of this makes you desperate for protection. A certain sense of despair is a necessary condition for taking sincere refuge. If you are in need and turn to someone or something which does not possess the capacity to protect you, you will find no help. You must know the qualities those you turn to should possess. They must be free from fear and skilled in helping others to become free from fear. They should be compassionate to all without bias and willing to help you whether or not you help them.

As a Buddhist one takes refuge in enlightened beings who possess these qualities, in their teachings and in the spiritual community of those who properly practice those teachings. Without any fear of suffering, you will not seek refuge and without any confidence in the Three Jewels or conviction that they can protect you, you will not entrust yourself to them. In *The Precious Garland* Nagarjuna[20] says:

From non-virtue comes all suffering
And similarly all bad rebirths;
From virtue all good rebirths
And every happiness in all lives.

Imagine that you are in terrible danger and someone who can rescue you appears. Your relief and joy are so great that you run to them as fast as you can and with complete trust fling yourself into their arms. Soundly based conviction that the Three Jewels can help you will bring immense relief and joy and make you want to take refuge at once.

Taking refuge in the Buddha means regarding him and all other enlightened beings as those who show you what your true refuge is. When you take refuge in the teachings, you regard their practice, particularly the attainment of nirvana, as your true protection because once you have freed yourself from cyclic existence you will never again experience suffering. When taking refuge in the spiritual community you regard its members as your role-models and friends.

You should know the distinguishing features of the Three Jewels and their particular qualities. Taking refuge entails making a sincere commitment to them in your heart and expressing it in words. The measure of having taken refuge is that you regard no other refuge as higher or ultimately more capable of protecting you. You undertake to observe certain specific and general precepts of training.[21] It is important to know these and to do your utmost to live by them. This prevents you from turning away from the Three Jewels and from allowing your commitment to decline, which has negative consequences in the future. Simply knowing the precepts but making no effort to keep them cannot protect you, but each time you make an effort to overcome a faulty way of thinking or acting and each time you try to develop or strengthen a good quality, you create your true protection. The Three Jewels can only help you if you do this.

Thinking about the infallible nature of the connection between actions and their effects, and putting into practice what you have understood is the way to avoid bad rebirths. To live in accordance with that natural law we also need to understand what makes actions powerful. Actions which are frequently repeated or motivated by strong feelings are powerful. A good action done out of faith, love or compassion or a negative action done out of anger, jealousy or lust is much stronger than a similar action done without these feelings.

Actions performed towards our spiritual teachers or parents and others who have been kind to us are weighty, as are actions performed in relation to those with good qualities such as the Three Jewels or towards those who are suffering. If virtuous actions are not destroyed by anger nor negative ones by some positive counteraction they remain powerful.

These considerations are important, since we want positive actions to be strong in every way and negative ones to be as weak as possible. For instance, a fellow worker keeps giving you tasks to do that are actually her responsibility. You feel annoyed and reluctant but nevertheless do them out of good manners. This creates virtue which will have good consequences. However since it falls into the category of an action which is performed but whose full karmic momentum does not accrue to you, the result is weak. Other actions which yield weak results are those intended but not performed, as, for example, when you mean to do something good but don't actually get around to doing it.[22] If you think of doing something positive, try to translate it into action as soon as possible with the best motivation. If you feel like doing something negative, try to refrain from carrying it out. When you have no option, at least insure that you do the negative action with reluctance and regret.

Observance of the natural law of karma begins with restraint from the ten harmful activities: killing, stealing, sexual misconduct, lying, the use of harsh language, the use of divisive language, idle gossip, covetousness, harmful thoughts and wrong views. When we feel convinced about the connection that exists between actions and their effects and try to live accordingly, we have discovered the correct worldly view. It is worldly not because it is relevant only to lay people.

Both lay and ordained people cannot practice effectively without adopting this view. The often-mentioned distinction between exalted and worldly is made from the point of view of direct perception of reality, which the exalted have gained and the worldly have not.

Your aim should be to protect your three gateways of body, speech and mind from faulty activity. If you perform any unwholesome actions, don't neglect to purify them. No matter how learned you are, nor what clairvoyant or miraculous powers you possess, you cannot afford to be careless about the actions you perform.

OUR TRUE CONDITION

Thinking about the suffering in bad rebirths helps to arouse the wish to find a way out of this cycle of involuntary birth and death, but for that wish to develop fully we must overcome our fascination with the marvels of cyclic existence. We can easily see how unstable and tenuous wealth, authority, power and fame are. The meteoric rise and fall of rulers, politicians, business magnates and film stars, whose activities make headline news for a short time, provide ample evidence of this. Though we know how ephemeral it all is, this is what attracts and fascinates us. Many of us, at least secretly, would like to be in their shoes, when the going is good! And if not exactly in their position, in one where we could enjoy more luxury and greater authority than we do at present. It is this compulsive attraction that must be overcome if we wish to escape from cyclic existence. We therefore have to force ourselves to consider the disadvantageous aspect of the very things that appear so compelling.

Everything associated with cyclic existence is fundamentally flawed. Birth as a human or celestial being is the best kind of birth in cyclic existence, but what does it herald, more pleasure or pain? Reflecting on certain facts helps our contemplation of the suffering associated with cyclic existence in general and with our human condition in particular. In his *Letter to a Friend* Nagarjuna speaks to his friend the king:

> Good one, develop repugnance for cyclic existence,
> The source of the many kinds of suffering, such as
> Lack of what you desire, death, sickness and ageing.
> At the cost of even your flesh, listen to its faults.

Of the eight kinds of suffering which characterize the dissatisfaction and misery of being human, Nagarjuna mentions only the suffering of ageing, sickness and death and that of not getting what we want, but we may also include in his "such as" the suffering of meeting with enemies, with what one does not want and of being parted from that which one loves. Finally there is the mere fact of having a contaminated body and mind.

We fail to recognize fully the misery of our own condition and need to be made aware of it by the teachings. It is worth sacrificing even our flesh for this, because unless we understand cyclic existence as a source of continual suffering, antipathy to it will not arise.

Aryadeva says:

> When there is no end at all
> To this ocean of suffering,
> Why are you childish people
> Not afraid of drowning in it?

The cycle of our rebirths is without beginning and is like a vast ocean of endless suffering in which we are drowning. This contaminated body and mind are cyclic existence as we experience it. Since time without beginning we have been floundering in this ocean, constantly made turbulent by sea serpent-like disturbing emotions and monstrous wrong views. We have been swallowed up by the vortexes of birth, sickness, ageing and death. When we are terrified of drowning in an ordinary sea whose breadth and depth can be measured, why are we not afraid of drowning for evermore in this wide and fathomlessly deep ocean? Is it because we have not noticed how great our suffering really is?

Suffering begins from the moment of conception, when consciousness, coming from a past life, is attracted to the ovum and sperm and enters the womb. In the Occident people imagine the womb as a comfortable and pleasant place, but in the Orient a rather different view prevails. The womb is seen as a dark and confining environment in which the fetus feeds off unclean substances like a dung-worm. If your mother ate something hot when you were in her womb, it felt as if fire was burning you. When she ate something cold, it felt as if you had been packed in ice. If she had a heavy meal, it was like being crushed by a mountain. Her sudden movements caused you intense pain and distress.

Could you bear to spend even a day squeezed into a copper vat full of sewage with the lid tightly closed? Or what if you were stuffed into a barely large enough foul-smelling jute bag and then its mouth was tied? The fetus is constricted for nine months with less and less room to move as the weeks go by.

At the end of that time, if you were fortunate as a result of positive past actions, you had turned upside down and were ready to make your way down the birth canal, but that does not always happen. Even under the best circumstances your entry into the world was traumatic, as you were forced through this narrow passage by your mother's contractions or pinched and pulled out by forceps. As a newborn baby you faced an abrasive environment. Even your first contact with air was painful. The gentlest handling, the softest clothes made you feel as if you had been thrust into a bundle of thorns. No wonder babies cry so much!

This is your story and not some fairy-tale Buddhists have invented. Unless you recognize it and feel a deep sense of abhorrence for this condition, you will never develop a strong wish for freedom. Even if you are still young, you must realize that youth will fade. The process of decline has already begun and its signs will shortly become apparent. It may seem distant to you now, but one day, and it won't be as long as you think, you will see the first grey hairs and unwanted wrinkles. Before you know what has happened, your bones are aching, you sit down like a sack of potatoes and it takes effort to rise. Your teeth break and fall out, your eyesight weakens and you have to peer hard or hold the printed page at arm's length to see anything without your glasses. You forget more than you remember. You can no longer get around the way you used to. You have to stop eating your favorite foods because you can't digest them. Is there a single item on this list of which you could say, "I like that! I'm looking forward to it"?

With a body of flesh and blood, sickness is inevitable and may well come before the grey hair and wrinkles. If it doesn't, it lies in wait. This body is composed of the elements—earth, water, fire and air—all four of which are essential since none of them alone can constitute the body. Unfortunately, however, these elements are hostile to one another and exist in a precarious state of balance which is called good health. As soon as any imbalance occurs, you feel unwell. Sickness makes your skin dry and slack. You begin to lose weight and your eyes look sunken. Instead of tasty food, which disagrees with you and aggravates your condition, you have to swallow medicines which taste bitter and unpleasant. Your bedside table is laden with bottles of pills. You endure painful injections, harrowing treatments and even the most radical surgery in the hope that you will recover.

With great anxiety you think about your condition, wondering if you will get better or worse. Eventually you realize that your illness is fatal and that you are going to die. You remember the mistakes you made, the hurtful things you did and the good you never managed to do. Time is running out and these memories fill you with regret. Now you must part from those you hold dear and from the possessions you have cherished. Though people may try to allay your fears by saying that death is just like moving from one house to another, whether or not you believe in rebirth, you are still faced with the question of what awaits you. Your anxiety makes you cry out and babble senselessly. As your faculties stop functioning you experience physical distress and this adds to your mental anguish.

Birth is associated with the trauma of the birth process, ageing with decline, sickness with the loss of well-being and death with separation, none of which we wish to experience. As well as these basic forms of suffering, we repeatedly encounter what is hostile and unwanted. Thieves may steal our property, weapons may be used against us, others may malign us or those in authority oppress us. We may be forced to live with people whom we detest and whose very presence makes us feel ill at ease.

We may also suffer separation from those we love and cannot bear to be without and from our dearest possessions. We may fail to obtain or accomplish what we want. Scholars frequently do not achieve the renown they desire. Monks or nuns cannot keep their vows of discipline as they intend. Celebrity eludes those who pursue fame and wealth eludes those who seek riches.

Simply having this contaminated body and mind is problematic because it is the basis for the suffering of birth, ageing, sickness and death. Since our attachment to it gives rise to disturbing emotions which make us act compulsively, it is like a magnet that attracts future suffering. It acts as the seed for the suffering of pain and the suffering of change and is itself the pervasive suffering of conditioning because only the slightest stimulus is needed for overt and intense suffering to arise. All this leaves little opportunity for us to enjoy happiness.

Change is painful and entails suffering when we try to cling to things which are by nature unstable and unreliable. However, not all change is associated with suffering. Study and practice of the teachings is intended to change us in a positive way but can only do so if we use the teachings for this purpose.

Great masters of the past have stressed the importance of contemplating the suffering of birth and the different aspects of the pervasive suffering of conditioning—the fact that anything conditioned and governed by compulsive actions and disturbing emotions is unsatisfactory and painful. These forms of suffering can only be understood properly if we have had some exposure to the teachings and have carefully examined our own experience. The other six kinds of suffering humans experience—ageing, sickness, death, separation from what we find attractive, encountering what we find unattractive, and seeking but not finding what we desire—are as self-evident as the pain a dog feels when it is hit by a stone. The dog doesn't need to give the matter any thought!

Ordinary people—those who have no direct perception of reality—are as unaware of the pervasive suffering of conditioning as you are of an eyelash in the palm of your hand. For the exalted—those who have perceived reality directly—that suffering is a constant irritant, like an eyelash in your eye. This body and mind are like a match, ready to burst into flame as soon as it is struck. It takes only a minor circumstance to provoke strong suffering.

Without contemplating and fully acknowledging our own suffering, we will never aspire to be free nor have true compassion for others. The Kadampa master Geshe Potowa says, "Once we have taken birth anywhere in the six realms, those who are going to be sick will be sick and those who are to die will die when illness, death and the like occur. This is neither unjustified nor has it happened by chance. It is the character or nature of cyclic existence and as long as we remain in cyclic existence it is unavoidable. If we feel an aversion to it, we must end birth and to do that we must get rid of birth's causes." Since suffering is endemic to our condition, astonishment and indignation when it occurs are inappropriate. Masters used to tell their disciples not to worry about getting rid of the sickness from which they were suffering but to think about getting rid of the causes which lead to birth itself.

Having thought about human suffering, reflect on the suffering experienced by gods and anti-gods despite their good rebirth. The gods possess fabulous wealth compared to the anti-gods who, tormented by envy, battle against them and suffer the ravages of war.

Nagarjuna speaks of the suffering experienced by the gods in his *Letter to a Friend*:

> It is said their body color turns ugly,
> They dislike their seats and their garlands grow old.
> Their clothes smell and hitherto absent
> Perspiration breaks out on their bodies.

Though the lives of celestial beings are full of pleasure and they do not suffer sickness and ageing, unpleasant signs appear as death approaches. Their beautiful appearance alters and they feel restless, unable any longer to enjoy the comfort of their elegant dwellings and seats. The garlands of flowers with which they adorn themselves, and which have always remained fresh, now wither and decay. They begin to perspire, particles of dirt adhere to their skin, and their silken robes, which have stayed clean and fragrant throughout their lives, become foul-smelling.

As death comes closer their radiance fades and their skin, which has never been wet because water rolls off it, needs to be washed and dried. Instead of the sweet rustle of silk and pleasant tinkle of jewelry, their clothes and ornaments emit unpleasant sounds. They begin to blink, a disagreeable sensation which they have never experienced during their celestial life. Instead of a general interest in all sense stimuli they become obsessed with one in particular.

Celestial beings are not all equally powerful, and those with greater dominion and wealth persecute, oppress and even drive out the minor gods. They sustain wounds in their battles with the anti-gods and these at times prove fatal. Since they know from which rebirth they have come, are aware of entering their present rebirth and can see where they will be reborn, they are referred to as those who can see three critical moments.[23]

The pleasures and luxuries they enjoy are the result of good actions they performed in the past, but without creating further virtue their stock of merit comes to an end and they are reborn in bad states. Not knowing what lies ahead makes us feel anxious and apprehensive, but the ability to see their unfortunate future clearly fills the gods with intense misery and fear.

Celestial beings in the desire realm are tormented by insatiable craving for sensual pleasure. No matter how much enjoyment they experience it is never enough, and obsession with pleasure prevents them from thinking of anything else. For this reason it is said that humans have a much better opportunity to develop a genuine wish for freedom and to gain insights.

Celestial beings in the form and formless realms, who are absorbed in blissful trance-like states of meditation as a result of their past actions, must take rebirth in lower states when the momentum of those actions comes to an end.

THE THOUGHT OF LIBERATION

Wherever we are born in cyclic existence, whether in good or bad states, suffering is our faithful companion. There are six kinds of suffering[24] which afflict us in all rebirths within cyclic existence. Uncertainty is the first. The very things which fascinate us, in which we place our hopes and to which we cling despite many disappointments are utterly untrustworthy and unreliable. Our friends, from whom we expect so much, may well have been our bitter enemies in past lives and vice versa. Those who are our friends now may become our foes later in life and our present foes may become our closest friends. A single word or look can change a relationship between morning and night. We join a friend for dinner, expecting to have a good time, and before the meal is over friendship has turned to enmity.

Just as drinking salt water cannot quench our thirst, no matter what we eat or drink or own, we never experience the expected satisfaction. The more we indulge, the more we crave. Our thirst for variety is never sated and as we pursue pleasure in the hope of fulfillment, we perform many negative actions which bring suffering. What we hope will still our hunger and bring gratification turns out to harm us. This lack of satisfaction is the second kind of suffering.

Through our ignorance we identify with a body formed from the sperm and ovum of others. Out of strong attachment to this body, which is quite unreliable and cannot last, we do much wrong. Despite our clinging and despite the time and energy we lavish on our troublesome body, we must relinquish it in the end and find a new one. This is the third form of suffering.

We cannot trust the glories of this world for there is constant flux between high and low, the fourth kind of suffering. The mighty fall from power and their subordinates take their places. The rich are reduced to penury overnight and the poor win the lottery. Everything changes.

The fifth form of suffering is that while we remain in cyclic existence we are alone and cannot depend on friendship. We spend some time with others, like guests in a hotel who stay for a while and then disperse in different directions, or like people who gather on market-day and then go their separate ways. Our friendships last just a short while. Shantideva says:

> When you are born, you're born alone
> And also when you die, you die alone.
> If others cannot share your suffering,
> What is the use of hindering friends?

We are born and die alone. In between we create much nonvirtue for the sake of our friends and loved ones, yet they cannot share the suffering this will bring us. We alone must bear it. Understanding the transitory nature of friendship, we should love and help those we call our friends without being attached to them and without letting our feelings for them hamper our spiritual practice.

The sixth kind of suffering is that we are conceived and born again and again. Each time we have to give up our body and begin once more. Unless we intervene this process will continue endlessly. When we gain direct perception of reality, the end of this cycle of involuntary birth and death is finally in view.

If you contemplate this brief summary of the many drawbacks of cyclic existence, it will encourage you to recognize your unique good fortune in having a sound body and mind. Your future well-being or misfortune depends on how you use them, so take care to make the right choice. What could be better than to devote your energy to developing these three principal insights, beginning with the wish to leave cyclic existence? This is the best way to make your life meaningful.

Sometimes when we read or hear the teachings, we may feel that there is so much to remember—eight of this, six of that and on and on. However, our memory has the capacity easily to store masses of facts. We absorb so much useless information from the media in the course of each day. If we see a practical application for what we learn from the teachings, all the better, since that will help us to retain and use it. But even if it does not seem immediately relevant, we can store what we learn for a time when it may come in useful. If we receive a precious gift, we feel happy and put it away carefully, even though we may not have any immediate use for it.

If, as it is said, just hearing the names of great masters like Asanga and Nagarjuna can protect us from bad rebirths, contemplating what they have written must surely provide greater protection. In his set of five treatises on the different levels[25] Asanga defines the three kinds of suffering[26] within which every kind of suffering can be included. He says the suffering of pain is that which is painful when it arises and while it lasts. That which is pleasurable when it arises and pleasurable while it lasts but is followed by pain when it stops, is the suffering of change. In fact everything impermanent that is produced through contaminated actions underlain by disturbing emotions is miserable and unsatisfactory.

Imagine you have a festering boil that has come to a head. When you pour cool water on it, you feel momentary pleasure. All contaminated pleasure and happiness is the suffering of change because the moment it stops, suffering of some kind starts. Asanga also views all mental activities and states of mind accompanying such contaminated pleasurable feelings as the suffering of change. The objects which induce these feelings are also included within this category of suffering because when they are removed, the pleasure ceases.

Now imagine that salt is rubbed into your boil or that something sharp touches its head. This creates intense overt pain. Contaminated painful feelings constitute the suffering of pain. When nothing cooling nor anything irritating comes in contact with the boil, neither pleasure nor outright pain occur. Contaminated neutral feelings are said to be the pervasive suffering of conditioning because they contain the imprints, causes and seeds for suffering and for the disturbing emotions.

All pleasurable feelings are not the suffering of change, since there are feelings of pleasure which are uncontaminated, such as the pleasure accompanying direct perception of selflessness. All pain does not necessarily constitute true suffering, the first noble truth. For instance, someone who has perceived reality directly and attained an uncontaminated path of insight may experience mental pain on realizing how much they still don't know. This pain is part of a true path and not an example of true suffering, since it does not result from contaminated actions underlain by disturbing emotions.

All neutral feelings are not the pervasive suffering of conditioning, since there are three kinds of neutral feelings: virtuous, non-virtuous and unspecified. Virtuous neutral feelings may be contaminated and uncontaminated. The latter are not an instance of the pervasive suffering of conditioning.[27]

The three kinds of contaminated feelings give rise to disturbing emotions. Pleasurable feelings arouse craving, while disagreeable feelings provoke anger. Neutral feelings lead to confusion which, for instance, wrongly takes what is impermanent to be permanent and what is unsatisfactory to be pleasurable. These disturbing emotions induce suffering. How obvious this is when craving makes us reach out for something whose attractiveness our incorrect mental approach has exaggerated! Unable to obtain what we have projected, which in reality does not exist, we suffer frustration and disappointment. This easily arouses anger, which is distressing now and creates future suffering. Confusion nourishes attachment and anger and makes us cling to suffering and its causes.

Practice focuses on interrupting the process by which feelings induce suffering. Instead of mistaking contaminated pleasurable feelings for real happiness, learn to recognize them as a form of suffering and stop attachment to them. When disagreeable feelings arise and you experience pain, try hard not to allow this to make you angry, by remembering that your body and mind are a mass of causes which produce suffering at the slightest provocation. To avoid the intense pain that comes when a head forms on the boil, you must deal with the boil itself. While you have a contaminated body and mind, pain cannot be avoided and will continue to occur.

From the Madhyamika viewpoint the three kinds of suffering are identified with painful, pleasurable and neutral feelings as described by Asanga. However, contaminated pleasurable feelings are not regarded as real pleasure but seen as a mere alleviation and diminution of suffering. They occur at the point when intense suffering of one kind has subsided and a new kind of suffering is beginning but has not yet become apparent. If this were real pleasure, it should increase as we continue to do what induces it. But we know that as we go on eating or indulging in other sensual pleasures, the feelings and sensations eventually become disagreeable. Suffering on the other hand is real because the more contact we have with what induces it, the more intense the suffering becomes.

Wherever we are born in the six realms with a body and mind which have resulted from contaminated actions and disturbing emotions, suffering is present. If you are carrying a heavy load, you can find no relief until you put it down. The surest sign that your body and mind hold the seeds of disturbing emotions and suffering is the fact that even the most minor circumstance can precipitate both.

In *The Three Principal Aspects of the Path* Tsongkhapa explains the practices of the initial and intermediate levels in relation to developing the wish to leave cyclic existence. In the contemplation of suffering, emphasis on stopping your own suffering leads to a strong wish to be free from the cycle of involuntary birth and death, whereas concern to stop others' suffering gives rise to compassion. How can you develop the great compassion wishing to free others from their suffering, unless you recognize, are moved by and want to be rid of your own suffering?

5

When through such familiarity not even a moment's longing
Arises for the marvels of cyclic existence,
And if day and night you constantly aspire to freedom,
You have developed the wish to leave cyclic existence.

As a result of repeatedly contemplating impermanence, the suffering of bad rebirths, the connection between actions and their effects and the suffering experienced in good rebirths, you come to see life in cyclic existence, even in the best celestial rebirth, as essenceless, and no worldly wealth, not even the fabulous riches of gods like Brahma and Indra, can tempt you.

A mother whose only child has gone missing can think of nothing else. Even her dreams are haunted by the longing to know what has happened and to hear some good news. This is her first thought on waking. When the thought of gaining liberation is, in the same way, foremost in your mind at all times, day and night, you have developed the wish to leave cyclic existence.

2 THE ALTRUISTIC INTENTION

THE PREDICAMENT OF SENTIENT BEINGS

With the intense wish for freedom from cyclic existence everything virtuous we do brings us closer to liberation, but without the altruistic intention it cannot become a cause for our highest enlightenment. Clairvoyant powers and the ability to perform miraculous feats do not become Mahayana qualities nor can they act as causes for peerless enlightenment unless they are backed by the altruistic intention.

6

Since this wish for freedom, if unaccompanied
By the altruistic intention, will not act as a cause
For the perfect happiness of unsurpassable enlightenment,
The wise arouse the supreme intention to become enlightened.

"Perfect happiness" refers to freedom from all the fears and dangers of worldly existence and those associated with the state of personal peace. Just the wish for freedom characterizes the practices of the intermediate level, but when this is combined with the altruistic intention, it becomes a path uniting the intermediate and highest levels of practice. Though Hearer and Solitary Realizer Foe Destroyers have freed themselves from the cycle of involuntary birth and death and possess qualities as great and precious as a mountain of gold, they cannot attain complete enlightenment because they lack the altruistic intention. The understanding of reality alone is not powerful enough to overcome the obstructions to knowledge of all phenomena. It can do so only when it is combined with skillful means.

In many sutras, such as the *Heap of Jewels Sutra,*[1] and in the great Indian treatises, such as *Engaging in the Bodhisattva Deeds* and the *Supplement to the Middle Way,* the importance of the altruistic intention is repeatedly stressed. To encourage yourself to develop it think about its many benefits.[2] If you were to churn the milk of the Buddha's teachings, the altruistic intention would be the butter. Once you develop it, both humans and celestial beings pay homage to you. Your presence brings happiness and well-being to the places where you live. The altruistic intention is a well-spring of both your own and others' good and a medicine that heals the troubles of the world. It dispels the dangers associated with remaining in a state of solitary peace.

Though your wisdom may not equal that of Hearers and Solitary Realizers, from the point of view of your family, you outshine them the moment you develop the altruistic intention because you have become a Bodhisattva. Even the smallest action performed with the intention to gain enlightenment for the sake of all living beings, such as giving a bird a few crumbs of bread, becomes the marvelous deed of a Bodhisattva. Virtue created with this underlying intention is inexhaustible. When anyone develops the altruistic intention, Buddhas rejoice as though a son or daughter has been born to them and they bless the new Bodhisattva. For other Bodhisattvas it is like the birth of a beloved sibling. The altruistic intention is the quintessential practice of all Bodhisattvas and the seed of all the magnificent qualities possessed by the enlightened ones.

If we feel bored by the description of these benefits, it is either because we do not believe in them, do not understand their implications or have heard them all before. The teachings are not intended as a source of entertainment or novelty but for practical application. Repetition helps us to remember so that we can then contemplate what we have learned in order to familiarize ourselves with it. First we must enrich ourselves by hearing and studying the teachings extensively. Shantideva says:

> If wishing to alleviate even just
> The headaches of living beings
> Endows you with limitless merit
> Because of your helpful intention,
>
> No need to mention that of wanting
> To rid each one of countless ailments
> And to convey each one of them
> To a state of limitless happiness.

If relieving a single ailment experienced by living beings creates great merit, how much more is created when we aspire to relieve the countless forms of suffering experienced by living beings without number and to give each one of them every possible kind of happiness. This wish and the willingness to take personal responsibility for doing so must come from the depths of our heart. Surely, whoever we are, we cannot but admire those who cherish such a wish. How amazing if each of our actions were governed by it!

7

Swept away by the strong currents of four great rivers,
Bound by the tight bonds of actions which are hard to escape,
Ensnared in the iron meshes of conceptions of a self
Beings are shrouded in thick darkness of ignorance.

To develop the altruistic intention think about how living beings, your mothers, are swept along by four swiftly flowing rivers. The torrent of ignorance consists of obstructions which can only be eliminated on the paths of seeing and

meditation.[3] The torrent of views comprises the false view of
the transitory collection as a real "I" and "mine," extreme
views, wrong views, considering misguided forms of discipline and conduct as supreme and holding faulty views as
supreme.[4] The torrent of desire includes all disturbing attitudes and emotions, other than ignorance and misleading
views, that are associated with the desire realm. Finally the
torrent of worldly existence consists of the disturbing emotions associated with the form and formless realms. These
causal torrents sweep living beings along, like a stick in the
strong current of a river, and lead to the resultant waters of
cyclic existence made turbulent by the irresistible currents of
birth, sickness, ageing and death.

Shantideva says:

> For Bodhisattvas even life-threatening danger
> Causes no wrong-doing but a natural growth of virtue.
> I pay homage to the bodies of those in whom
> Has arisen this precious and holy state of mind.
> I take refuge in those who are a source of happiness,
> Who ally you to happiness, even when harmed.

Even when their lives are threatened, Bodhisattvas, whose
concern for others is so firmly rooted that it far outweighs
any concern they might have for their own well-being and
safety, do not respond angrily or otherwise destructively but
turn the situation into a source of virtue. Let alone not thinking of revenge, they find ways of caring for those who harm
them and of leading them towards true happiness. For Bodhisattvas events of this kind are opportunities to purify
negativities and create merit. Even in their sleep they constantly accumulate merit through their supreme altruism. We
can become like them if our wish is strong enough and we
are prepared to make sufficient effort.

Living beings, our very kind mothers, are not merely swept
along by these currents of cyclic existence, into which they
are born involuntarily through the force of disturbing emotions. It is as though their hands and feet are tightly bound

by the bonds of their past actions. These are difficult to throw off, hamper them and cause them untold suffering. They are ensnared in a net of iron meshes, caged in a steel cage of misconceptions regarding the self.

If you were plunged into a fast flowing river in this condition during the day, someone on the river bank might see you or hear your cries for help, but on a dark and lonely moonless night you would be invisible and your cries would go unheard. Our mothers are helpless and cannot even recognize what will bring them happiness, let alone find the way to freedom.

Imagine being in a pitch-black room which you know to be infested with scorpions. The fact that you cannot see makes it all the more frightening. Unable to see their true condition, confused living beings harbor all kinds of misconceptions which lead to actions that bring them further suffering.

8

Endlessly born in worldly existence, and in those births
Incessantly tormented by three kinds of suffering—
Reflecting on the condition of your mothers
In such a predicament, arouse the supreme intention.

When we reflect sufficiently on how living beings are helpless and constantly tormented by the suffering of pain, of change and by the pervasive suffering of conditioning, we will recognize our responsibility towards them. How can we call ourselves Mahayana practitioners, if we ignore their state and look the other way? If we do nothing, the promises many of us make regularly as part of our daily prayers, calling upon Buddhas and Bodhisattvas to be our witnesses, are just hollow.

Pitying others who suffer is not enough. We must train ourselves in the special wish to take personal responsibility for their well-being. This goes counter to our natural inclination to turn tail and leave it to someone else! Once we are willing to accept this responsibility, we have to acknowledge that at present it is not in our power to help others by the most effective means and that to do so we must gain enlightenment. This is how the altruistic intention arises.

First gain an understanding of the process and then follow it. Reflect on how living beings lack happiness until an intense loving wish to give them happiness comes as naturally as the ever-present thought of food when your stomach is empty. Think about their suffering until the compassionate wish to free them from it grows so strong that it is constantly in your mind, just as a mother whose only child is sick can think of nothing but finding a cure for it. Love and compassion must become powerful enough to influence everything you do. Only such love and compassion will arouse the special wish to take personal responsibility for others' happiness that leads directly to the altruistic intention.

Thinking about how living beings lack happiness and endure suffering will only move us to love and compassion if we feel close and connected to them. The closer we feel to any person or animal and the more affection we have for them, the less we can bear to see them suffer, whereas we feel no compunction about seeing those we dislike suffer. Their unhappiness may give us satisfaction and we may even wish worse disasters on them. From this it is apparent that affection which regards all living beings as lovable is essential for developing great love and compassion.

Many of the well-known texts contain good explanations of how to develop the altruistic intention. Two techniques which are particularly effective are explained clearly by Tsongkhapa in his *Great Exposition of the Stages of the Path*. They are known as the "seven cause and effect instructions"[5] and "equalizing and exchanging self and others."[6] While there are other equally good explanations of how to employ these methods, I am familiar with Tsongkhapa's and will draw on that.

If you wish to paint a fresco, you must first prepare a smooth and even wall surface which will accept the paint well. The foundation for both the above-mentioned approaches is equanimity. Leveling the ground of our feelings is the initial step because at present that emotional ground is made rough and uneven by attachment and aversion.

Equanimity in this context is not just a wish for all beings to live in a state of harmony, uninfluenced by attachment and hostility which cause them suffering. Here your main concern is to rid yourself of prejudice which makes you attached to some and hostile to others. Such a wish is not exclusive to practitioners of the Great Vehicle but is also cultivated by Hearers and Solitary Realizers. Going beyond this and wishing equally to free all others from suffering and give them happiness is a form of equanimity unique to the Great Vehicle.

Having established such equanimity, you can follow either route leading to the development of affection which sees all living beings as lovable. Both approaches converge at this point, from where you then go on to develop great compassion, the special wish and the altruistic intention.

It may take you months, years or a whole lifetime to develop a single one of these insights. Even if you were to die tomorrow, it would be worth learning and practicing today. If you lack the necessary supportive conditions, you may fail to develop any insights despite your perseverance, but your efforts will not have been wasted because they will bear fruit in the future. It is like leaving something precious for safekeeping with a friend when you set off on a journey—something that you will retrieve on your return.

In the *Illumination of the Thought*,[7] his commentary on Chandrakirti's *Supplement to the Middle Way*, Tsongkhapa says, "Those who put effort into training themselves in great compassion, both through greatly cherishing living beings in their hearts and through thinking about their suffering in cyclic existence, make Chandrakirti's uncommon homage meaningful. Otherwise, assuming that one knows about these things is just like a parrot's imitation." Here Tsongkhapa stresses the importance of combining heartfelt concern for others with contemplation of their suffering to arouse compassion.

The stronger your compassion for living beings, the greater urgency you will feel to attain enlightenment for their sake. Conversely, if your compassion is weak, your altruistic intention will also lack intensity. Your own concerted effort as well as the blessings derived from making sincere requests to your spiritual teacher, regarded as indistinguishable from Avalokiteshvara, the embodiment of enlightened compassion, and whose mind you imagine as inseparable from your own, will enable you to develop great compassion.

You may wonder if great compassion only occurs after the affection which sees all living beings as lovable has been developed and before the special wish arises. Chandrakirti says in his uncommon homage to compassion:

> Since compassion itself is seen as the seed
> Of a Victorious One's rich harvest,
> As water for its growth and as
> Ripening into a source of long enjoyment,
> I therefore first bow to compassion.

In the Tibetan tradition of Buddhism those who have any knowledge of the Indian master Chandrakirti's works revere him as an inspiring teacher and practitioner of both sutra and tantra. With these words he draws attention to the importance of compassion at the beginning, in the middle and at the end. It is essential initially because it makes us resolve to free living beings from suffering. Intermediately, when we are Bodhisattvas, it enables us to persevere with the many difficult tasks which must be performed for the sake of others. Finally, when we are enlightened, the force of our compassion makes us continue working for the good of living beings rather than remaining in a state of peace as do Hearer and Solitary Realizer Foe Destroyers.

Tsongkhapa's *Illumination of the Thought* also says, "If you want to be a Mahayana practitioner, you must gain a firm conviction in the necessity of training yourself in what [Chandrakirti] has explained—you should recognize that your mind must first be governed by great compassion; then, dependent upon this, that you must arouse the altruistic intention to attain enlightenment, complete in every respect, from the depths of your heart and that, having done so, you must engage in the practices of Bodhisattvas in general and in particular gain utter certainty regarding the profound view."

LEVELLING THE GROUND

To develop compassion and the great affection for living beings which gives rise to it, a sense of closeness with them all is essential. At present we feel affection and compassion for our parents, children, partners and friends, but these are biased feelings, restricted only to those we like, while we lack sympathy for those we dislike and are unaffected by their suffering.

When attempting to develop equanimity, we must rid ourselves of attachment to our loved ones, which is not to say that we must give up our affection for them. However, since our feelings of love and compassion are mixed with clinging and craving, our aim must be to distill these feelings until they are pure. Developing greater equanimity is the essential basis and preparation for this, like limbering up.

Begin cultivating it by vividly evoking someone who is neither your friend nor foe. Imagine not only their appearance but also their way of speaking and moving. As you do this observe your feelings. Probably no strong feelings of attachment or aversion will arise because this person is and does nothing that is either particularly agreeable or disagreeable to you. If you notice any attachment or aversion, calm and let go of it. Even with such a relatively mild feeling this is quite difficult to do.

Often people think that equanimity means feeling nothing, but it is in fact a very agreeable feeling. We are so accustomed to strong emotions that we feel anesthetized when there is no intense affect. Observe your feelings when attachment and hostility die down. You may discover an unfamiliar sense of peace. Unless you can gain this emotional evenness, true compassion and love will elude you.

Attachment, craving and desire on the one hand and anger, aversion and hostility on the other upset our inner equilibrium and make our mind rough and unworkable. Anger is certainly not a comfortable emotion because its distressing effects are quickly felt both mentally and physically. Desire and attachment seem pleasurable at first, but they excite and agitate us in ways which soon cause discomfort.

When you have gained some familiarity with a feeling of equanimity free from attachment and hostility towards the neutral person whom you imagined before you, vividly imagine two more people. On one side of the neutral person is someone you love dearly and on the other someone you heartily dislike. Don't allow these three persons to appear as lifeless cardboard cutouts. Watch your feelings as you consider the person you like. Why do you like them so much? Probably because he or she has been kind to you and helped you or done what you wanted. And why do you dislike the other? Because he or she has harmed or offended you in some way. Try to make the feelings of attachment and aversion which surface die down until you have the same feeling towards these two as you have towards the neutral person. Consider that the person you like now has harmed you in past lives and that the one you dislike has previously helped and supported you.

Meditating on these three people in the way described may lead directly to feelings of equanimity towards all living beings. However, you may also need to remind yourself that all living beings suffer and lack happiness yet none want suffering and all long for happiness. They are totally alike in this, so why be prejudiced in favor of some and against others? We resist these thoughts because we feel comfortably familiar with our entrenched emotional habits—our attachments, our aversions and our indifference.

When trying to recognize all living beings as your mothers, consider what the great master Dharmakirti explains in his *Commentary on the Compendium on Valid Cognition* about the beginningless nature of awareness. Think first how today's awareness is a continuity of yesterday's awareness and that this year's awareness is similarly a continuum of the previous year's. Retrace awareness in this way, reflecting on the fact that this life's awareness is a continuity of your previous life's awareness. It is thus impossible to find a point where awareness began. Nor can you find any beginning to your cyclic existence and therefore to your births.

You cannot say with certainty, "I was never born here," for you have been born everywhere, in every place many times. If this is so, you also cannot say, "I was never conceived in this being's womb," for you have been conceived in every womb and every single being has been your mother, not just once but numerous times.

Another approach may also be used. Imagine your mother of this life before you, exactly as she is at present, young or old. This is undeniably your mother. Then consider that she has been your mother many times before. The Buddha, whose words for very sound reasons are considered trustworthy, frequently spoke of the previous lives of those he encountered and said that his mother, who gave birth to him in Lumbini, had been a mother to him in many other lifetimes.

When you have gained conviction that your mother of this life was also your mother countless times before, try to recognize that your father, your brothers and sisters, your friends and even your foes have also been your mothers in other lives. Gradually extend this recognition to include all living beings. When you can quite naturally regard them as your mothers, you have accomplished the first step.

Now think about the kindness of all these motherly living beings. Begin by contemplating your present mother's kindness. When she realized that she was pregnant with you, she took particular care of her health, remembering your well-being when she chose what to eat and drink. She was conscious of how her movements might affect you and tried not to do anything abrupt or anything that could endanger you. For nine months she nurtured you in her womb, constantly aware of your presence there. Your birth caused her considerable pain, yet when she held you in the palms of her hands, a tiny vulnerable baby, she was as overjoyed and delighted as if she had found the most precious, breathtakingly beautiful treasure.

What were you like as a newborn baby? Like a tiny insect on its back, you waved your arms and legs about helplessly, unable to do anything for yourself. Newborn babies are often red and wrinkly, but in your mother's eyes you were the most adorable thing on earth. She held you to her heart, nourished you with her milk, called you by the sweetest names she knew, gazed at you lovingly and removed the dirt from your body with her hands, not even thinking of it as dirt because of her great affection for you. You could not return her affection but were as insatiable as a little fledgling with its beak wide open waiting to be fed.

As you grew and began to crawl, she protected you from all kinds of dangers and taught you everything essential—how to eat, how to control your bowels, how to walk and talk. She sent you to others to learn what she could not teach you herself. Although you don't remember it now, she was once the center of your world and your favorite place was her lap. You clung to her, followed her around, called her again and again to attract her attention, asked her hundreds of questions and howled if she was out of sight for more than a few minutes. No one could console you as she could, when you had an accident, got upset or felt sick.

At least for a time your birth robbed her of vigor and beauty. When you grew up she gave you her possessions and used her savings that she was reluctant to spend on herself for you. You took all this for granted and at the same time you probably rejected any authority she may have had over you.

Such has been your mother's kindness in this and other lives, that she has preferred to be sick and even die herself rather than to see you suffer. Thinking about her kindness is not intended to make you feel guilty or to increase attachment but to arouse appreciation. It is possible to think, "my mother" with warmth and affection but without any sense of possessiveness. All living beings have shown you such kindness repeatedly, not only as human but also as animal mothers. Recognizing and acknowledging that kindness, allow a strong sense of gratitude and a wish to repay the kindness of living beings, your mothers, to arise.

Think how they are swept along by the irresistible currents of the disturbing emotions and attitudes which carry them into the turbulent waters of cyclic existence, where they are tossed on the waves of birth, sickness, ageing and death, constantly prey to the three kinds of suffering.

Imagine that your mother is in great danger, from which you can protect her but instead you ignore her. How despicable! When you are in a position to help living beings who cannot help themselves, can you in good conscience turn your back on their suffering? Providing food and drink for the hungry and thirsty, medical treatment for the sick, and serving those who need assistance addresses their immediate needs. You may help someone who is ambitious to gain a position of influence and authority. This satisfies their worldly needs, but perhaps you have actually added to their suffering. Helping others requires much wisdom and the very best form of help is to show them the way to gain inner freedom and enlightenment.

All living beings want happiness yet lack not just the supreme happiness of enlightenment but even the most ordinary kinds. The very pleasures they mistake for happiness are in fact the suffering of change. Though they yearn for happiness, they don't know how to create its causes and instead do the opposite by creating the causes of more misery.

Think of repaying the kindness of living beings by alleviating all the suffering they experience, from the mildest to the most intense, and by giving them every form of happiness, including the highest. Think, "Why shouldn't they enjoy happiness and its causes? May they enjoy happiness and its causes! May I help them to do so!" and "Why shouldn't they be free from suffering and its causes? May they be free from suffering and its causes! May I help them to be so!"

Repeatedly cultivating equanimity, the recognition of all living beings as your mothers, recollection of their kindness and the wish to repay that kindness from the depths of your heart naturally gives rise to the affection which sees all beings as lovable. No other specific practice is necessary for this. The subsequent compassion and love should be so strong that they can induce the special wish to take personal responsibility for others' well-being. It is not enough just to wish others happiness. You must be prepared to step in and help them achieve it. Compassion is like the eye, love like the hand and the special wish like the shoulder, for without it you cannot shoulder the burden of others' well-being.

How can you tell whether or not you have developed the affection that sees all living beings as lovable? If a person or creature is sick and you don't care, it is a clear sign that you do not find that living being lovable. When you really feel like reaching out to give an affectionate hug to all the people and animals you encounter, no matter what they are like, you have developed the affection that sees them as lovable. Once we have reached that stage the rest is easy.

Geshe Potowa had a natural concern for others from the earliest age and even as a child, watching groups of travellers passing near his home, he wished that they might journey in peace together and meet with good fortune. Once when he was very small he saw the wind driving the autumn leaves along and thinking that they were little creatures being swept away against their will, he began to cry. Later in life he said he could not remember ever having had a selfish wish or thought!

A Radical Shift

The seven cause and effect instructions demand that you think about past lives. The approach of equalizing and exchanging self and others does not initially require this and may therefore be a more comfortable route to take for those who have difficulty with the idea of reincarnation. At present our attitude towards ourselves and our attitude towards others are far from equal. We are extremely concerned with our own well-being and very little concerned with theirs. In fact, however, they are no different from us because they want happiness and no suffering just as much as we do. "Equalizing self and others" means developing as great a concern for them as we have for ourselves.

"Exchanging self and others" does not involve thinking of them as us and us as them but switching our habitual attitudes and priorities. In the past we have been almost exclusively concerned with our personal happiness and problems. Now we resolve to focus our concern on bringing others happiness and alleviating their suffering. Hitherto we have neglected them. Now we resolve to neglect our own interests by putting them second. These changes in outlook are brought about by considering the many drawbacks of egocentricity and the many advantages of cherishing others. Concern for ourselves is so ingrained and habitual that a word is enough to upset us. Can such an instinctive attitude be changed? Shantideva assures us that it can:

> Don't give up because it is difficult.
> It is like this: though hearing his name
> Filled you with fear, through the force of habit
> You will feel unhappy when he is absent.

When an enemy, the mere mention of whose name once filled you with fear and loathing, becomes your close friend, you grow so accustomed to his presence that you miss him and feel unhappy when he is absent. A complete reversal has taken place and now even just hearing his name gives you pleasure.

Our self-concern is the source of all our miseries. Shantideva says:

> Since whatever violence there is in the world,
> The many kinds of fear and suffering,
> All come from the conception of a self,
> What use is this great demon to me?

"I... I..." is constantly present in our minds. The different anxieties, fears and phobias, the physical violence and the illnesses we experience are all rooted in our self-centeredness. Our exaggerated sense of self and our compulsion to find happiness for this larger-than-life self we have fabricated cause us to ignore, neglect and harm others. Of course, it is our right to love and take care of ourselves, but not at the expense of others. While "As long as I'm alright" is our motto, we have no hesitation in acting with total disregard for others.

We may find this description of self-concern altogether too crass to apply to us. "I'm not like that," we object, but though we may not consciously think in this way, when self-concern is operating, our behavior shows a cold indifference to others. Conflicts between partners, parents and children and with other family members, conflicts between students and teachers and on a larger scale within and between countries have their source in personal and collective self-concern. We will never overcome our misconceptions of the self and our egocentricity until we fully recognize how destructively they affect us.

Buddhas and Bodhisattvas see clearly that our neglect of others, our self-preoccupation and our disregard for the connection between actions and their effects are responsible for all our miseries. The feeling that it doesn't matter what we do as long as we can get away with it kills our chances of liberation and enlightenment. Our selfishness robs us of worldly and supramundane good qualities, leaving us naked and empty-handed. It separates us from happiness now and in the future and fetters us to suffering.

Resolve never again to let yourself be dominated by this mean and selfish way of thinking and do everything in your power to combat it. Your happiness begins the moment you recognize self-cherishing as your chief foe. There are many good reasons why cherishing others makes sense. Shantideva says:

> The state of Buddhahood is accomplished
> Equally through living beings and Victorious Ones.

> What kind of behavior then is it to revere
> Victorious Ones but not living beings?

The past kindness of living beings is our focus when we think about what they have done for us while they have been our mothers. In training ourselves to exchange self and others we also think about their kindness to us at other times.

They are like wish-granting jewels because we rely on them for everything we want and need, both in a worldly and spiritual sense. Our very survival depends upon them. How would we get food, clothing and shelter without them? This good human body and mind are the result of observing ethics in relation to them. Whatever prosperity we enjoy has come about through our past generosity to them. We cannot practice the teachings or attain enlightenment in a vacuum, but only with their help.

Since they are of paramount importance to us, we should give them the highest respect and esteem, no less than we do to a deity or to our spiritual teachers. If we truly want to please Buddhas and Bodhisattvas and all those noble beings in the world whom we admire and whose sole guiding principles are their affection, love and compassion for others, we can do nothing better than to cherish living beings.

Shantideva says:

> Whoever quickly wants to protect
> Themselves and others
> Should practice the holy secret
> Of exchanging self and others.

He also says:

> All the happiness in the world
> Comes from wanting others' happiness.
> All the suffering in the world
> Comes from wanting your own happiness.
> What need is there to say a lot—
> The childish act for their own good.
> Subduers act for the good of others.
> Look at the difference between the two!
> If you do not sincerely exchange
> Your happiness for the suffering of others,

You will never attain Buddhahood.
In cyclic existence there is no happiness.

This teaching of exchanging self and others is a secret for those who lack the courage to go against the conventional opinion that one's own well-being is of primary importance and that everything one does should be aimed at insuring it. People guided by this idea are incapable of envisaging such a radical switch in attitude and do not realize that their compulsive preoccupation with personal comfort and well-being is the source of all their troubles, while all happiness and everything good in this world results from cherishing and helping others.

We have spent countless lifetimes relentlessly pursuing happiness but have still not succeeded in securing it and unwillingly continue to suffer. Enlightened beings, on the other hand, have gained their extraordinary qualities by completely devoting themselves to others. Until we consider others' well-being more important than our own and until we can neglect our own personal interests instead of neglecting others, we will stay imprisoned in cyclic existence, deprived forever of peace and happiness.

To familiarize oneself with these new attitudes and to strengthen love and compassion, it is customary to practice giving and taking. With the warmth of affection for living beings in your heart, consider how they lack the happiness for which they yearn and with intense love send them your own happiness and the virtue which acts as its cause. Imagine that this gift satisfies them in every way, providing them temporary happiness, including that of good rebirths, as well as the ultimate happiness of liberation and enlightenment. Don't think of what you will get out of such generosity, but dedicate even the merit created by it to their well-being.

Now contemplate how all living beings are afflicted by many kinds of suffering, and with intense compassion for them imagine taking it as well as the actions and disturbing emotions which cause them misery. Draw this in and direct it into your heart, where it destroys the selfishness heaped there.

As you become familiar with using your imagination in this way, giving and taking can be done as you exhale and inhale. According to the oldest texts the practice consists of giving and taking in this order, but many masters recommend that you should take away the suffering before you give happiness with the rationale that when someone is experiencing intense suffering, they cannot enjoy the gifts you give them. Even the best food or clothing will not make them forget their pain.

As you take on the suffering and its causes, make a heartfelt wish that these may ripen on you and destroy everything negative in yourself—your self-centeredness, your own emotional or physical sickness and pain. As a practitioner of mind training, when you are sick or disturbed by strong emotions, you make the wish that your suffering may replace the suffering of others. The suffering, karmic forces and disturbing emotions which you take on do not remain in your body and cause you harm but are dissipated in the course of this. If you do the practice with sincerity and courage, you will definitely not be adversely affected by it.

It is vital not to misunderstand the point of these practices or what is meant by the negative aspects of self-cherishing. Do not use your ingrained self-concern as a reason for self-hatred or low self-esteem. Though you may feel completely identified with your self-centered impulses at present and it may seem that your disturbing emotions are an integral part of your character, you do not need to remain under their sway but can free yourself from them.

We are entitled to happiness and should cherish ourselves, but we must know how to do it in the right way. As long as we consciously or unconsciously exploit others, our quest for happiness will be in vain, but if we use ourselves liberally for others' happiness, we will never again be the losers.

When doing the practice in conjunction with breathing, imagine living beings before you and draw out their suffering and its causes, which leave from their right nostrils and coalesce into a black beam. This enters your left nostril, striking and destroying everything negative within you. Then, as you exhale, send out a white light bearing happiness and its causes. This leaves through your right nostril and enters their left nostrils. Do this during seven or eight inhalations and exhalations. Quality is more important than quantity, since the practice is intended as an expression and strengthening of love and compassion and should not be done automatically without any feeling. Whatever your spiritual tradition, this practice can find a place within it and will prove only beneficial.

If you feel you are being harmed by human or non-human beings, think about how in past lives they were your very kind mothers. Because they were preoccupied with protecting you from harm and doing everything they could for your happiness, they never engaged in spiritual practice and performed many negative actions. For this reason they are suffering now and act harmfully because they do not know any better. They are blind to the repercussions of their present negative actions and to the closeness of their relationship to you. Something about you, perhaps simply the way you walk or talk, provokes them to harm you. Recognize your own role in this.

Instead of retaliating, imagine taking on their suffering and giving them happiness. Try to do what you can to help them and to stop their destructiveness. This may be too difficult at present, since our natural instinct is to have as little contact as possible with those who harm us, but at least try to wish them happiness and freedom from suffering. If even this seems beyond you, just say words which express that wish to accustom yourself to them. In his *Precious Garland* Nagarjuna says:

> May their wrong-doing ripen on me
> And may all my happiness ripen on them.

Strengthening love and compassion through the practice of giving and taking leads to the special wish, the commitment to take responsibility for others' well-being. You might think,

"Why do I need to take on this responsibility? Surely that's what Buddhas and Bodhisattvas are supposed to do." This is an unworthy thought. It's like thinking that your sister or brother, your cousin or some other family member will look after your mother when she is ill and that you don't need to bother. If you are fully aware of what your mother has done for you and are grateful, you will not only feel obliged to play your part but will want to as a way of repaying her kindness.

Similarly when you make the special wish, you firmly resolve not to cast around for others who will take responsibility but promise to do all you can yourself to alleviate the suffering of others, to give them happiness and ultimately to lead them to complete enlightenment. Looking honestly at your own present capacities, you have to admit that you are quite unable to do this. Let alone taking care of all living beings, you probably find it hard to take proper care of even one. Perhaps you feel barely able to take care of yourself.

Only enlightened beings have abilities which are commensurate to the task of helping countless other living beings. By becoming enlightened you fulfill your own highest potential and help others to fulfill theirs. Each one of your physical, verbal and mental activities then satisfies the needs of limitless living beings.

If you are very thirsty and want to drink some tea, you need a cup to hold it. Like the thought of something to drink, the main objective of the altruistic intention is others' good. Your own enlightenment is simply the expedient means by which this may be accomplished.

In his *Abridged Stages of the Path*[8] Tsongkhapa says of the altruistic intention:

> The altruistic intention is the mainstay of the supreme vehicle,
> The foundation and basis of its powerful activities.
> Like an elixir that turns the two stores to gold,
> It's a treasure of merit comprising every kind of good.
> Knowing this, heroic Bodhisattvas make this precious

And supreme attitude their quintessential practice.
I, the practitioner, have done this
And those who seek liberation should do likewise.

Only the altruistic intention can turn the extensive activities of Bodhisattvas into the great stores of merit and insight that yield enlightenment. It alone transforms the practices of giving, ethical discipline and so forth into perfections and makes the vast virtue created by Bodhisattvas into an inexhaustible treasury. Knowing this Bodhisattvas make cultivation of the altruistic intention their central practice.

You might think that you already have the altruistic intention because you recite words expressing it as part of your daily practices, but words are not enough. When you strongly wish from the depths of your heart to attain enlightenment for the sake of others, you have developed the aspiring altruistic intention. At this point you enter the Mahayana paths of practice and begin to create the great stores of merit and insight which take three countlessly long aeons to amass.

When you make a formal commitment never to relinquish the altruistic intention until you become enlightened, you must refrain from four negative or black activities, engage in four positive or white ones and observe the precepts associated with the aspiring altruistic intention.[9] If you still feel unready to make this commitment, simply arouse the altruistic intention again and again. Once your aspiration is firmly established, you are ready to take the Bodhisattva vow[10] by which you promise to engage in the extensive deeds of Bodhisattvas. This is the engaged altruistic intention.

You know that you have actually developed the altruistic intention when the urge to become enlightened is constantly present and you feel that the suffering of living beings in cyclic existence, particularly in the bad states of birth, is so intolerable that you must attain enlightenment as quickly as possible. Once the altruistic intention has arisen in this way, you must keep familiarizing yourself with it and train yourself to observe the precepts which strengthen it and prevent it from declining.

3 THE CORRECT VIEW

MISCONCEPTIONS

While the Buddha and the great masters who came after him repeatedly praised the correct understanding of reality as seminally important, they also reiterated that the profound view of the Middle Way[1] is extremely hard to find. Without it the key factor which gives life to the practices of sutra and tantra is missing. If we misunderstand the Middle Way by mistaking lack of inherent existence to mean non-existence, we plunge into an abyss of nihilism which endangers our future, since this error encourages us to act irresponsibly by disregarding the connection between actions and their effects.

Only someone who has thought profoundly about what the "absence of intrinsic existence" means could come to the mistaken conclusion that it refers to total non-existence. There is little risk of this for most of us, since we do not give much thought to how things exist and cling firmly to their true existence. Familiarity with the philosophy of the Middle Way may make us adept at using its terminology. Phrases like "empty of inherent existence" and "not truly existent" roll glibly off our tongues, while actually we assent and hold fast to the objective and independent existence of things. At present we cannot distinguish between existence and true existence, nor between lack of inherent existence and non-existence, except verbally.

Unless we establish for ourselves the non-existence of even the most subtle object of negation or impossible mode of existence to which we adhere, and if we continue to take things to be in any way truly or inherently existent, we hold a view of reified existence or eternalism which simply reinforces the misconceptions that imprison us in cyclic existence.

There are four systems of philosophical tenets in Buddhism which superficially appear to contradict each other but which actually lead to progressively subtler levels of understanding. They are like the essential rungs of a ladder which allow us to reach the supreme understanding of reality. Each of us needs to use all the rungs. These systems of thought with their gradations of subtlety represent the various approaches the Buddha used to teach about different levels of reality to those at different levels of understanding. His underlying intention was to lead everyone in the most appropriate way towards the profoundest understanding of reality, that everything is free from the extremes of reified existence and total non-existence.

This understanding of the most fundamental way in which things exist is difficult for us to gain because we lack sufficient merit from the past. Moreover we take little interest in creating such positive energy now because we do not recognize the important role this understanding plays. Many of us also lack sufficient intelligence and the acquired faculty of thinking analytically which are needed to gain insight into reality. Even though in the Buddha's day more people possessed the necessary positive energy, intelligence and philosophical acumen, the Buddha at first believed that the true nature of reality would be too difficult to understand, and therefore he remained in seclusion without teaching for some time after his enlightenment.

9

Though familiar with the wish to leave cyclic existence
And with the altruistic intention, you cannot cut the root
Of worldly existence without wisdom understanding reality,
So make effort in the means to comprehend dependent arising.

The wish to leave cyclic existence and the altruistic intention cannot counteract the misconception of the self which is the root of cyclic existence. This can only be destroyed by the correct understanding of reality, without which one cannot progress further than the Hinayana or Mahayana path of accumulation. This profound view of the Middle Way opens up all paths and stages and is like a sighted guide who can lead blind pilgrims to their destination. Having resolved to free living beings from cyclic existence, we must gain this understanding, for we cannot help them through kindness alone. Knowledge of the best means grows out of this crucial understanding.

Even the correct worldly view regarding the connection between actions and their effects, itself grounded in the correct supramundane view, the understanding of reality, cannot free us from cyclic existence. The *King of Meditative Stabilizations Sutra*[2] says that even if we develop the eight concentrations of the form and formless realms, they will not enable us to get rid of the disturbing emotions nor even effectively to decrease them. Practices such as giving or the observance of ethical discipline cannot free us either, no matter how dedicated we are. Only the understanding of selflessness can cut the root of this repeated cycle of involuntary birth and death and only by familiarizing ourselves with it can we attain nirvana. In *Yogic Deeds of Bodhisattvas* Aryadeva says:

> There is no other door to peace,
> And it destroys wrong views.
> That which is the object of
> All Buddhas is called selflessness.

The understanding of emptiness is the most powerful agent to clear away our suffering, its causes and all non-virtue. It dispels the obstacles created by the disturbing emotions and makes room for compassion and love to grow.

Yet this understanding of selflessness lacks sufficient power unless it is combined with love and compassion. The *Vimalakirti Sutra*[3] says:

> Our aim is to fulfill our highest potential by attaining the wisdom truth body of an enlightened being and to fulfill the needs of others by attaining the form bodies of an enlightened being.[4]

Nagarjuna, Chandrakirti and other great masters concur that this is possible only through uniting wisdom and skillful means to amass the great stores of insight and merit. Chandrakirti says that the conventional, the altruistic intention to attain enlightenment for the sake of all living beings, must function in unison with the ultimate, the understanding of reality. With these two we can reach the state of a Victorious One's perfected qualities, just as a bird with two healthy wings can soar in the sky.

How is the understanding of selflessness gained? Begin by regarding your spiritual teacher as inseparable from Manjushri, the manifestation of enlightened wisdom, and make sincere prayers of request that you may succeed in understanding reality. When the earth is warm in springtime, seeds begin to sprout. Similarly the warmth of your spiritual teacher's blessings prepares the ground for the seed of hearing and studying the teachings on reality to sprout and grow. Following Tsongkhapa's illustrious example, purify your wrong-doing and obstructions by acknowledging them according to the *Sutra of the Three Heaps*[5] and by doing prostrations. Also create positive energy by offering the mandala[6] and performing the seven-part practice.[7]

Then study the Perfection of Wisdom sutras and the commentaries on them by Nagarjuna and his spiritual sons, Aryadeva and Chandrakirti, which describe the nature of reality. Acquaint yourself with the terminology and methods of reasoning used to establish the fundamental nature of everything that exists, so as first to acquire a sound intellectual understanding. The biographies of renowned past masters tell us that this is what they did.

You must become aware of how the misconception of the self is responsible for your disturbing emotions and faulty actions. Investigate how it views the self. From the habitual sense of an exaggerated "I" which is automatically present comes a strong sense of mine, expressed in terms of "my body," "my mind," "my things," "my country" and so on. This leads to emotions of clinging attachment and hostility, giving rise to actions that bring unwanted suffering.

Until you fully recognize the harm done by this misconception, you will not wish nor make any effort to get rid of it and so will never understand selflessness. Examine closely how the misconception functions, how it perceives the object on which it focuses and how it causes disturbing emotions to arise.

Many types of misconception regarding the self exist, some of which result from speculation about its nature or from adherence to particular philosophical views, but here we are concerned with our instinctive and innate misconception of the self. This focuses on the validly existent self and distorts it in such a way that it is held to be truly or inherently existent. It regards the self not as something merely attributed but as an independent entity with objective existence. The misconception of the self is operative when the self not only appears to have true existence but we assent to that appearance. The truly existent self—something entirely non-existent—to which the misconception clings is the object of negation.

Identify this fabrication clearly by allowing that self to appear so vividly that you feel you could reach out and touch it. Unless you take the trouble to evoke it properly, your meditation on selflessness will be like shooting an arrow without having a target. It will be like locking the door when the thief is climbing through the window or doing rituals to repulse harmful spirits at the west door when they are entering from the east.

Since you want to understand emptiness in order to free yourself from suffering and since this entails tackling your fundamental misconception of the self, everything hinges on properly identifying what you are searching for.

The four schools of philosophical tenets[8] posit the object of negation differently. Their assertions begin with the coarser levels of fabrication and end up with the most subtle. For the Vaibhashikas the self which is negated is a permanent, single, independent entity—permanent in that it does not change moment by moment; single in that it does not have parts; and independent in that it does not depend on causes and conditions.

For Sautrantikas the self which is negated is more subtle. They assert that the person is an imputation and that the object of negation is a self-sufficient substantially existent self.[9]

For Chittamatrins, who hold that forms and the awarenesses which perceive them both result from the same imprint and are not different entities, any kind of external existence or existence independent from the perceiving awareness is the object of negation. For the Svatantrika branch of the Madhyamika school, who contend that everything exists both from its own side as well as through being posited by a non-defective awareness, existence exclusively from a thing's own side without being thus posited is the object of refutation. For the Prasangika branch of the Madhyamika school, who maintain that all things are mere attributions, any kind of existence that is not posited by awareness is the object of negation.

All these schools of thought employ the reason of dependent arising to refute their specific object of negation. The Vaibhashikas, Sautrantikas and Chittamatrins, who are proponents of true existence, use the reason of dependence on causes and conditions. This, however, only establishes the dependently arising nature of impermanent but not of permanent phenomena, namely those which do not undergo change from moment to moment. Svatantrikas use in addition the reason of dependence on parts, which applies to both permanent and impermanent phenomena, while Prasangikas add dependence on a basis of attribution and on the attributing thought. This most subtle level of dependence cannot serve as a means to induce understanding of emptiness, since it is only understood fully once emptiness has been cognized. It is most fruitful, therefore, to concentrate your efforts on thinking about the generally accepted aspects of dependent arising— dependence on causes and conditions and on parts.

Contemplating the dependently arising nature of all produced phenomena associated with the person, body and mind, referred to as internal phenomena, and of all external phenomena in terms of their dependence on causes and conditions and on parts helps us to gain greater confidence in the connection between actions and their effects, protects us from a nihilistic view and indirectly leads us closer to the understanding of emptiness. Though there have been other great spiritual teachers in the world, the Buddha is incomparable because he taught about interdependence, namely that everything existent is a dependent arising.

10

Whoever sees that the causes and effects of all phenomena
In cyclic existence and beyond are unfailing
And thoroughly destroys the mainstay of misconceptions,
Walks on the path that pleases the Buddhas.

The words "all phenomena in cyclic existence and beyond" indicate the bases of emptiness, while the words "the causes and effects of all phenomena are unfailing" indicate the reason of dependent arising which disproves the existence of "the mainstay of misconceptions," true existence.

Everything that exists from forms to omniscience depends on parts and, where impermanent phenomena are concerned, on causes and conditions. The presentation of the unfailing nature of causes and their effects is incontrovertible. True existence, the mainstay of our misconceptions, is demolished by the reason of dependent arising, for nothing has ever existed truly and objectively. When you understand that not an atom of true or inherent existence can be found anywhere and that, at the same time, causes and effects as well as actions and agents operate perfectly, you walk the path which pleases the enlightened ones.

Since the root of cyclic existence is the misconception of the self, to free yourself you must first be convinced of selflessness and then gain a profound understanding of it. Selflessness can be established using diverse approaches, but here Tsongkhapa focuses on the reason of dependence and emphasizes particularly that everything which exists does so in dependence upon a basis of attribution and a process of attribution by name and thought. Nothing exists in and of itself independently of these factors.

For instance, the person or self certainly exists as the agent of actions and the experiencer of their results, happiness and suffering. If you hold that the self does not exist at all, you ascribe to a nihilistic view. Certain schools of thought identify the self, which can be benefitted and harmed, with consciousness. Some specify that it is mental consciousness while others assert it is the foundational consciousness.[10] Prasangikas hold that the self is merely attributed to the body and mind. Since mind, particularly mental consciousness, is a subtler phenomenon with more stable continuity than the body, the self is primarily attributed to it.

The self depends on causes and conditions and on parts and does not exist objectively and independently as appears to the misconception of the self. It is attributed by name and by thought to its basis of attribution, the body and mind. It is in no way independent of such naming and conceptuality. This applies equally to the body and mind that serve as the basis of designation for the person. The body itself is attributed by name and concept to a basis of attribution consisting of a collection of body parts. The mind is an attribution to a collection of mental functions and moments of mental activity.

You may wonder whether this intellectual understanding of reality is essential or whether perhaps there is some other practice which leads more directly to the actual experience of emptiness. The fundamental nature of things is a subtle phenomenon, which at this point we are unable to perceive in the way that we perceive visible objects with our eyes. In order to apprehend it we must first learn about it and gain knowledge derived from study. Then we must think extensively about what we have understood and investigate in order to clarify doubts and confusion. When our understanding has become sound, we familiarize ourselves with it repeatedly to gain the wisdom derived from meditation.

In Buddhist practice there are two broad kinds of meditation—analytical and placement meditation. Both kinds must be employed even in the cultivation of love and compassion. First you arouse these feelings strongly by thinking about the plight of living beings and then you experience and sustain the feelings during placement meditation. When they fade, you induce them again through analytical meditation.

DEPENDENCE AND ATTRIBUTION

Everything the Buddha taught was intended for practice. If you fail to see intellectual understanding as a part of practice and seek instructions for practice elsewhere than in the words of the Buddha, something has gone badly awry. You know from experience that both positive and negative inner changes can be brought about by the power of thought, so do not underestimate its positive potential.

The more closely you examine and think about something which accords with fact, the clearer it becomes, whereas that which has no basis in reality vanishes. For instance, if you mistake a distant scarecrow for a man and look through your binoculars to get a clearer view, you will see only a scarecrow and your perception of a man will cease. If there really were a man on the opposite hillside, he would become clearer the more closely you look.

Our misconception of the self, which distorts what exists, is the source of our suffering. The more we investigate to see whether the object to which this misconception clings actually exists, the more evident its non-existence becomes and gradually the misconception dies away. When we gain a direct perception of reality as the result of this process, we become exalted beings, a source of refuge for others and worthy of their homage. The Buddha encouraged us by saying that he had practiced and become enlightened and if we do likewise, we can become enlightened too. We have the same potential that he had.

Can choice exist in a world of dependently arising and conditioned things? In fact if things were not dependent on causes and conditions, choice would be precluded, but their very dependence permits our choices to create causes and conditions which set in motion new chains of dependent arising. This gives us hope, since it indicates the definite possibility of personal transformation if we create the causes and circumstances that allow it to take place.

You may wonder whether, if there are multiple choices, different possible futures already exist. Your future exists but not now, otherwise you would already be old. You can prepare for a long life by making certain choices regarding your life-style, diet and the like, but you cannot be certain that you will live to an old age because all the necessary causes and conditions must be in place for a particular result to occur. If even one is missing, the sought-for result cannot come into being.

Expressing the reason of dependent arising as a syllogism, one could say, "All phenomena in cyclic existence and beyond are free from even the slightest inherent existence, the mainstay of conceptions of true existence, because they arise dependently." Anything which depends on other factors cannot exist in and of itself. Take the appointment of a professor for example. This first requires someone who is suitable for the job. An uneducated and retarded individual cannot perform the function of a professor. Then a valid act of designation must take place. The person is not a professor until he has been appointed to that post. Otherwise it would follow that he should have been a professor as a baby from the moment of his birth, indeed even while he was still in his mother's womb.

Before he receives the title of professor, he will not think of himself as a professor and nor will anyone else, but once he has been appointed, he will think, "I'm a professor," and others, for instance those working in his department, will think of him as such.

Although the dependent nature of this example seems obvious, it is actually quite subtle. Everything that exists depends on such a process of designation by name and concept. Horses and elephants, houses and mountains all exist in this way—as mere attributions. Nothing has true or objective existence.

If everything is merely attributed, why can't you call brass gold and gold brass or an ox an elephant and vice versa? Although everything is merely attributed, for the process to be authentic the basis of attribution must be able to perform the function of that which is attributed to it. The attribution must satisfy three criteria: it should appear to conventional awareness, and it should not be invalidated by any other valid conventional perception nor by awareness investigating the ultimate nature of things.

For instance, someone looking at a scarecrow on the other side of the valley mistakes what he sees and says to you, "Look at that man over there on the hill." You look where he is pointing and agree, "Yes, I can see the man," and to your perception it is a man. But then another person, who has just come from there, says, "That's not a man. It's only a scarecrow." His valid conventional perception contradicts and invalidates the attribution you have made.

The first two features, however, are not sufficient to insure the validity of what is designated. The attribution must also be unharmed by awareness investigating the ultimate. For instance, if one designated an objectively existent table to the basis of designation, this would certainly appear to conventional perception and would not be contradicted by any valid conventional perception, but would be invalidated by awareness investigating the ultimate. This awareness, however, does not invalidate the mere designation "table" to the four legs and flat top.

Every validly existent attribution fulfills these criteria. Though things have no ultimate or true existence, they exist conventionally. If anything had ultimate or true existence, it could not depend on any other factors, but since everything depends on its basis of attribution, nothing has objective or true existence. Again and again sutra and tantra mention that all phenomena are dependently attributed, that they are free from the two extremes and are empty and selfless.

When a search is made for the object of refutation, for instance, for an objectively existent table, which is how the table appears to exist, it cannot be found. Unfindability here indicates the absence not of the table but of an objectively existent table. All Buddhist schools of philosophy other than the Prasangikas assume some kind of objective existence which is found when the imputed object is sought. For Prasangikas findability of any kind would imply true or objective existence, which they negate.

The most pertinent area of concern for us, however, is the self. When no investigation is made, the self clearly exists, as in "I am sitting" or "I am eating." There are only two ways in which the self could exist—either it is dependent or independent. To us it appears to exist entirely from the side of our body and mind, independent of any process of attribution, but if it existed as it appears, it should be findable when we search for it, either within the body or mind or as something separate from these. It should become more and more apparent as we proceed with the investigation.

There are several points to consider when investigating whether the self is the body. If the self were the body, it would cease when the body is cremated at death. Just as there are many body parts there should be many selves. Furthermore, it would be impossible to say "my body," which expresses the relationship of what to us appears as a controller and that which is controlled. Just as the master is not the servant, the self is not the body, yet the self is not an entity apart from the body either. If it were, it would be impossible to speak of "my body." A horse and a cow are different entities. When the cow is sick, you cannot say that the horse is sick, but when your body is unhealthy, you say, "I am sick" and when it is healthy, you say, "I am well." The self and the body are thus in a dependent relationship.

If the self were the mind or consciousness, since the self appears to exist independently without relying on other factors, consciousness should also exist independently. However, consciousness cannot arise without an object. Pleasurable and unpleasurable states of mind depend upon attractive and unattractive objects. A single moment of mentation depends on many causes and conditions. For instance, a moment of visual awareness depends upon the presence of a visible form, the eye sense faculty, space between the two and a preceding moment of awareness.

As in the case of the body, the fact that we say "my mind" is an indication that self and mind are not identical, yet no self can be found distinct from the mind. When we experience anxiety and mental tension, we say, "I am unhappy," and when we are in a positive and joyful state of mind, we say, "I am happy."

Does the self exist? Yes, but not as we perceive it. Why does it appear to exist but cannot be found when we search for it? Because it is false: it appears to be what it is not and exists in a way which does not accord with how it appears. Yet owing to our confusion and imprints of ignorance we assume that it exists as it appears.

In Buddhist literature selflessness is mentioned repeatedly. We must understand correctly to what this refers and what kind of self does not exist. In his commentary on Aryadeva's *Yogic Deeds of Bodhisattvas* Chandrakirti succinctly formulates what is meant by self and selflessness: "Here 'self' is an inherent nature of phenomena, that is, a non-dependence on another. The non-existence of this is selflessness." The self is very clearly dependent on its basis of attribution, on the process of attribution, on parts and on causes and conditions and thus has no inherent existence. Identifying the object to which the misconception of the self adheres is of supreme importance because to us it appears to exist—as something independent and not merely attributed to body and mind.

Ahead of you on the path lies a coiled mottled rope, but you are not aware of this. Darkness is falling. As you stroll along, you suddenly see a snake in front of you and halt in terror. The snake appears from the side of what is lying on the path. It appears to exist in and of itself and you assent to this appearance, which causes fear to arise. The snake is a figment of your imagination, a fabrication and the object of negation, but you cannot be sure of this until you make an exhaustive search for it where it appears.

When someone calls your name, you respond by thinking, "Oh! he's calling me." The "I" which appears to your mind at that moment is the validly existent self. But if that same person then accuses you of theft and you are innocent, you will feel defensive, self-righteous and your "I" will swell in size, appearing much larger than when your name was called. It will seem quite independent of any other factors. In normal situations the appearance of the fabricated self is difficult to identify but in situations of crisis it pops up vividly. The nominally attributed self exists as a mere attribution and a mere appearance and when no investigation is made it functions satisfactorily.

The appearance of a truly existent self exists and the self which seems inherently existent to the misconception also exists. What does not exist is a truly or inherently existent self. When you start to realize the absence of that self, you have begun to find the correct view and to "walk on the path that pleases the Buddhas." If you then nurture this understanding, you will eventually see that nothing has even an atom of true existence.

On the level of appearances, as mere attributions to causes and conditions and to parts, things are functional and actions and agents operate faultlessly, but if you are not satisfied with this and try to pinpoint things under examination, nothing can be found. This unfindability indicates lack of inherent existence. The statement that things are mere attributions and mere appearances should not be taken as a denial of their existence.

The reflection of the face in the mirror undoubtedly exists but is not what it appears to be—a real face. Even though it is in every respect not what it seems to be, the reflection is not non-existent but exists and functions satisfactorily because with its help you can put on makeup or attend to blemishes. This is how all things exist and the fact that they lack ultimate existence does not predicate their non-existence.

The greater your understanding of dependent arising, the more convinced you will be about the connection between actions and their effects. You will respect it because you recognize that through the natural law of dependent arising positive actions yield agreeable results and negative ones disagreeable results. The understanding of dependent existence reveals the absence of inherent existence, while understanding that things are not inherently existent confirms the connection between actions and their effects and the dependently arising nature of everything associated with cyclic existence and the state beyond.

Through the dependent nature of things a seed can produce a sprout. If the seed were inherently existent, the sprout could never be produced. If youth had inherent existence, old age would never occur and if sentient beings were truly existent, they could never become Buddhas. But youth depends on the presence of causes and conditions as does old age. And, fortunately for us, we are not inherently existent and can therefore free ourselves from habits, which at present seem impossible to break, and gain undreamed-of qualities.

When the view of reality has been perfected, lack of inherent existence and dependent arising are clearly seen to support each other, but until then, when the one is clear and apparent, the other is not.

11

So long as the understanding of appearances
As unfailing dependent arising and of emptiness
Free from all assertions seem disparate,
You still do not comprehend the Subduer's thought.

The understanding of the dependently arising and unfailing way in which causes and conditions produce their effects is a cognition of conventional reality, while the understanding that everything is empty of true existence is a cognition of the ultimate mode in which things exist. The way in which these two understandings apprehend their objects differs. So long as they seem incompatible and your understanding of a thing's dependently arising nature appears to undermine your understanding of its emptiness of true existence and vice versa, you still have not gained insight into what the Buddha intended to reveal nor have you found the correct view of the Middle Way. This is an indication that you must continue to persevere.

APPEARANCE AND EMPTINESS RECONCILED

12

When the two do not alternate but are simultaneous,
And merely seeing dependent arising as unfailing
Destroys through certainty how the object is perceived,
Analysis with regard to the view is complete.

Eventually, when this disparity ceases and you can reconcile the dependently arising nature of things with their emptiness of true existence, and appearance and emptiness come together in such a way that you can posit both simultaneously with regard to a single object, you have ascertained the correct view. You understand that things exist as mere nominal imputations and that virtue produces happiness and non-virtue suffering, yet when the imputed object is sought, no form of objective existence can be found. These two aspects—appearance and emptiness of intrinsic existence—characterize everything that exists. Now you recognize and apprehend them together.

Through the force of your understanding of the unfailing way in which things arise dependently, the fabricated object to which the misconception clings is destroyed. The understanding of emptiness and the understanding of dependent arising have a reciprocally strengthening effect, through which it becomes ever clearer that the self, while lacking all intrinsic existence, is a viable agent of actions and experiencer of results.

In the tenth verse Tsongkhapa speaks of thoroughly destroying "the mainstay of misconceptions." In the eleventh verse he mentions emptiness "free from all assertions." In the twelfth verse he refers to an understanding which "destroys through certainty the way the object is perceived." These phrases may be variously interpreted. "The mainstay of misconceptions" is generally viewed as true existence itself.[11] The qualification of emptiness as being "free from all assertions" may be taken to mean that words cannot describe emptiness as it is. It can also refer to emptiness free from any assertions of intrinsic existence. Some early masters in Tibet, who subscribed to the Madhyamika view that everything is empty of inherent existence, found it difficult to posit conventional existence. They contended that since all phenomena are empty, they cannot be specified as this or that, as either existent or non-existent, and that proponents of the Middle Way hold no position, since they propound emptiness free from all assertions.

The third line of the twelfth verse has been read as meaning "destroys through certainty the way the object is perceived," namely that the very understanding of everything as arising dependently and as merely attributed to a basis of attribution induces certainty regarding lack of inherent existence and thus demolishes true existence and the mode of apprehension which clings to true existence.

On the other hand, this line may be read as meaning that the understanding of dependent arising "destroys the way the object is perceived with certitude." Both any possibility of true existence and the certitude with which true existence is perceived are destroyed by the understanding of dependent arising.

These different interpretations by past masters are possible because the Tibetan is extremely succinct. Although a legal code, for instance, should be as clear-cut as possible to avoid ambiguity, from a Buddhist point of view it is considered an advantage if a text is open to various interpretations. This is seen as a mark of its profundity and the exploration of differing exegeses can extend and enrich our understanding.

13

Further, when you know how appearances preclude the extreme
Of existence and emptiness precludes the extreme of annihilation
And how emptiness appears as cause and effect,
You will never be enthralled by wrong views.

All Buddhist schools of philosophy other than the Prasangikas see appearances as precluding the extreme of non-existence and emptiness as precluding the extreme of reified existence. Here, in a way unique to the Prasangika school, mere appearance dependent on many factors is seen as precluding the existence of things from their own side, namely reified existence, while emptiness of inherent existence signifies their reliant nature and therefore precludes their non-existence. The very fact that things exist dependently means they cannot be other than empty of inherent existence. Like an old man who clearly cannot manage on his own because he depends on the help of his stick, things cannot exist in and of themselves because they exist dependently. Those who assert true existence accept the dependence of products on causes and conditions. For them this dependence confirms the true existence of these products rather than refuting it. Svatantrikas accept that in addition to dependence on causes and conditions, everything existent depends on its parts and they affirm that nothing has true existence. Nevertheless they assert that things have a degree of existence from their own side.

Do those who believe in a creator accept the dependently arising nature of things? Perhaps they would say that everything in creation is a dependent arising because it depends on the creator. But on what does the creator depend? If there is anything which is not dependent, it should be truly existent, but nothing can exist in this way.

For Prasangikas the understanding of dependent arising goes hand in hand with the understanding of emptiness. Emptiness is like the source from which all conventional phenomena appear. In their diversity they are like manifestations of emptiness. Once you understand this, wrong views like those of reified existence or nihilism can never enthrall you. Because things are empty of inherent existence, it is possible to posit the operation of causes and effects and the connection between actions and their consequences. Emptiness, out of which they arise, facilitates their existence. Causes that are empty of inherent existence produce effects equally empty of inherent existence. Even though we assent to this view on an intellectual level, we continue to experience things as inherently existent and respond to them as such.

The reason of dependent arising is said to be the king of reasons because it demolishes both extremes. In the statement "the seedling is not truly existent because it is a dependent arising" the words "is not inherently existent" specify the object of negation, thereby making it clear that the existence of the seedling is not in question. They convey that the seedling is not non-existent but exists as something dependent. The reason "because it is a dependent arising" tells us that the seedling not merely exists but exists as something dependent and is therefore not inherently existent. This approach differs from the more usual interpretation mentioned before, in which lack of inherent existence precludes the extreme of reified existence and dependent arising the extreme of non-existence.

"Is not inherently existent" alone precludes both extremes by explicitly excluding reified existence and by indirectly affirming dependent existence, which excludes non-existence. "Dependent arising" by itself similarly precludes both extremes in that the word "dependent" excludes inherent existence and the word "arising" excludes non-existence. The interrelationship of the two—emptiness and dependent arising—is clearly indicated by the words of the *Heart Sutra*, "Form is empty and emptiness is form."

When the correct understanding of reality is accompanied by a strong wish for personal freedom from cyclic existence, it becomes a cause for liberation. When accompanied by the altruistic intention it leads to complete enlightenment. Whether one is a practitioner of the Hearer, Solitary Realizer or Great Vehicle, this understanding is indispensable, which is why emptiness is regarded as the mother of all exalted beings.

14

When you have correctly understood
The essentials of these three principal paths,
Child, seek seclusion and strengthen your effort
To swiftly accomplish your future well-being.

Tsongkhapa concludes with kindly encouragement to practice. When you are thoroughly familiar with the essential points regarding the wish to leave cyclic existence, the altruistic intention to attain enlightenment for the sake of all living beings and the correct understanding of reality, you must overcome your attachments and seek seclusion. Unless you reduce your physical busyness, cultivate contentment and limit your desires, you cannot practice effectively. Seeking seclusion is not simply a matter of physical isolation. Your mind is like a city densely populated with thoughts. Seeking seclusion also involves quieting the chatter of mental busyness and becoming immune to the eight worldly concerns.

Enthusiastic effort means taking a delight in virtue. If that joy is absent, practice simply becomes strenuous and fatiguing. Effort directed towards non-virtuous activities, no matter how joyful, is not enthusiastic effort in the Buddhist sense. Our future well-being refers to all the conditions we require for our happiness and development from now till we attain enlightenment. With affection Tsongkhapa urges us to act swiftly, since we do not know how long this precious opportunity will last.

To avoid discouragement he tells us to strengthen our enthusiastic effort. When we undertake studies, we are often in a hurry to gain extensive knowledge and recognition. When we begin a retreat, we secretly hope for visions and signs. These hopes and expectations will almost certainly be dashed and prove an obstacle to the very things we wish to attain. Remembering that the Buddha Shakyamuni spent three countlessly long aeons amassing the great stores of merit and insight necessary for his enlightenment, we should have the persistence to spend as long as it takes, even many lifetimes, to bring about inner change. Our aim should be to make small changes day by day.

Kadam Geshe Dolpa said we should be farsighted, broadminded and relaxed.[12] The farsighted vision of complete enlightenment for the sake of all living beings requires a broadminded approach, namely the willingness to invest as much time and effort as is needed to accomplish this aim by practicing according to the three levels of capacity and according to the stages of generation and completion of tantra. In the world it is considered sensible and wise to make long-term plans and to work hard to insure a secure old age, even though we have no idea how long we will actually live. When it comes to spiritual practice, which has more lasting implications, we choose the shortest and easiest practices. With such an approach how can we hope to accomplish anything great? We must dedicate our tremendous unused potential to the task of transforming ourselves now.

Despite this sense of urgency we should be moderate and relaxed in our attitude to practice. It is important to know oneself and how much one is capable of doing in good spirits. Short bursts of intensive formal practice punctuated by periods when practice is forgotten are not fruitful. It is much better to practice in moderation continuously. If our state of mind is spacious and relaxed, we will not suffer from nervousness, anxiety and depression. Practice done without joy does not bring good results.

The colophon says:

This was taught to Tsako Wönpo Ngawang Drakpa by the learned and fully ordained monk, the glorious Losang Drakpa.

The teaching on the three principal paths was given by Tsongkhapa at the request of Tsako Ngawang Drakpa[13] who was one of Tsongkhapa's earliest disciples to attain distinction. He practiced in seclusion for long periods and was free of pollution by worldly concerns and activities.

The commentary which forms the main source for this oral teaching was compiled by Losang Dorje and is based on five teachings which he received on Tsongkhapa's text from the great master Pabongka Rinpoche.[14] These three principal paths are explained in many great works, since they are quintessential Buddhist practices. If we understand Tsongkhapa's short text well, we can approach other explanations with confidence and use them to enrich our understanding.

Root Text

The Three Principal Aspects of the Path
by Je Tsongkhapa

Homage to the venerable and holy teachers!

1

I shall explain as well as I can
The essence of the Victorious Ones' teachings,
The path praised by their excellent children,
The gateway for the fortunate seeking liberation.

2

Unattached to the joys of worldly existence,
Striving to use well their freedom and riches
Trusting the path that pleases the Victors—
Fortunate ones, listen with a pure mind.

3

Without the wish for freedom there is no way to calm
The pursuit of pleasant effects in the sea of worldly existence.
Since those with bodies are fettered by their thirst for being,
First seek the wish to leave cyclic existence.

4

Freedom and riches are hard to find; life is fleeting—
Familiarity with this stops clinging to this life's pleasures.
Repeatedly considering actions, their unfailing effects
As well as the suffering of cyclic existence
Stops clinging to future pleasures.

5

When through such familiarity not even a moment's longing
Arises for the marvels of cyclic existence,
And if day and night you constantly aspire to freedom,
You have developed the wish to leave cyclic existence.

6

Since this wish for freedom, if unaccompanied
By the altruistic intention, will not act as a cause
For the perfect happiness of unsurpassable enlightenment,
The wise arouse the supreme intention to become enlightened.

7

Swept away by the strong currents of four great rivers,
Bound by the tight bonds of actions which are hard to escape,
Ensnared in the iron meshes of conceptions of a self
Beings are shrouded in thick darkness of ignorance.

8

Endlessly born in worldly existence, and in those births
Incessantly tormented by three kinds of suffering—
Reflecting on the condition of your mothers
In such a predicament, arouse the supreme intention.

9

Though familiar with the wish to leave cyclic existence
And with the altruistic intention, you cannot cut the root
Of worldly existence without wisdom understanding reality,
So make effort in the means to comprehend dependent arising.

10

Whoever sees that the causes and effects of all phenomena
In cyclic existence and beyond are unfailing
And thoroughly destroys the mainstay of misconceptions,
Walks on the path that pleases the Buddhas.

11

So long as the understanding of appearances
As unfailing dependent arising and of emptiness
Free from all assertions seem disparate,
You still do not comprehend the Subduer's thought.

12

When the two do not alternate but are simultaneous,
And merely seeing dependent arising as unfailing
Destroys through certainty how the object is perceived,
Analysis with regard to the view is complete.

13

Further, when you know how appearances preclude the extreme
Of existence and emptiness precludes the extreme of annihilation
And how emptiness appears as cause and effect,
You will never be enthralled by wrong views.

14

When you have correctly understood
The essentials of these three principal paths,
Child, seek seclusion and strengthen your effort
To swiftly accomplish your future well-being.

This was taught to Tsako Wönpo Ngawang Drakpa by the
learned and fully ordained monk, the glorious Losang Drakpa.

༄༅། །ལམ་གྱི་གཙོ་བོ་རྣམ་གསུམ་གྱི་རྩ་བ་བཞུགས་སོ།།

རྗེ་བཙུན་བླ་མ་རྣམས་ལ་ཕྱག་འཚལ་ལོ།

༡ །རྒྱལ་བའི་གསུང་རབ་ཀུན་གྱི་སྙིང་པོའི་དོན།
།རྒྱལ་སྲས་དམ་པ་རྣམས་ཀྱིས་བསྔགས་པའི་ལམ།
།སྐལ་ལྡན་ཐར་འདོད་རྣམས་ཀྱི་འཇུག་ངོགས་དེ།
།ཇི་ལྟར་ནུས་བཞིན་བདག་གིས་བཤད་པར་བྱ།

༣ །གང་དག་སྲིད་པའི་བདེ་ལ་མ་ཆགས་ཤིང་།
།དལ་འབྱོར་དོན་ཡོད་བྱ་ཕྱིར་བརྩོན་པ་ཡིས།
།རྒྱལ་བ་དགྱེས་པའི་ལམ་ལ་ཡིད་རྟོན་པའི།
།སྐལ་ལྡན་དེ་དག་དང་བའི་ཡིད་ཀྱིས་ཉོན།

༣ །རྣམ་དག་ངེས་འབྱུང་མེད་པར་སྲིད་མཚོ་ཡི།
།བདེ་འབྲས་དོན་གཉེར་ཞི་བའི་ཐབས་མེད་ལ།
།སྲིད་ལ་བརྐམ་པ་ཡིས་ཀྱང་ལུས་ཅན་རྣམས།
།ཀུན་ནས་འཆིང་ཕྱིར་ཐོག་མར་ངེས་འབྱུང་བཙལ།

༤ །དལ་འབྱོར་རྙེད་དཀའ་ཚེ་ལ་ལོང་མེད་པ།
།ཡིད་ལ་གོམས་པས་ཚེ་འདིའི་སྣང་ཤས་ལྡོག
།ལས་འབྲས་མི་བསླུ་འཁོར་བའི་སྡུག་བསྔལ་རྣམས།
།ཡང་ཡང་བསམས་ན་ཕྱི་མའི་སྣང་ཤས་ལྡོག

༥ །དེ་ལྟར་གོམས་པས་འཁོར་བའི་ཕུན་ཚོགས་ལ།
།ཡིད་སྨོན་སྐད་ཅིག་ཙམ་ཡང་མི་སྐྱེ་ཞིང་།
།ཉིན་མཚན་ཀུན་ཏུ་ཐར་པ་དོན་གཉེར་བློ།
།བྱུང་ན་དེ་ཚེ་ངེས་འབྱུང་སྐྱེས་པ་ལགས།

༦ །དེས་འབྱུང་དེ་ཡང་རྣམ་དག་སེམས་བསྐྱེད་ཀྱིས།
 །ཟིན་པ་མེད་ན་བླ་མེད་བྱང་ཆུབ་ཀྱི།
 །ཕུན་ཚོགས་བདེ་བའི་རྒྱུ་རུ་མི་འགྱུར་བས།
 །བློ་ལྡན་རྣམས་ཀྱིས་བྱང་ཆུབ་སེམས་མཆོག་བསྐྱེད།

༧ །ཤུགས་དྲག་ཆུ་བོ་བཞི་ཡི་རྒྱུན་གྱིས་ཁྲིར།
 །བཟློག་དཀའ་ལས་ཀྱི་འཆིང་བ་དམ་པོས་བསྡམས།
 །བདག་འཛིན་ལྕགས་ཀྱི་དྲ་བའི་སྦུབས་སུ་ཆུད།
 །མ་རིག་མུན་པའི་སྨག་ཆེན་ཀུན་ནས་འཐིབས།

༨ །སྐྱེ་མེད་སྲིད་པར་སྐྱེ་ཞིང་སྐྱེ་བ་ར།
 །སྡུག་བསྔལ་གསུམ་གྱིས་རྒྱུན་ཆད་མེད་པར་མནར།
 །གནས་སྐབས་འདི་འདྲར་གྱུར་བའི་མ་རྣམས་ཀྱི།
 །དངངས་ཚུལ་བསམས་ནས་སེམས་མཆོག་བསྐྱེད་པར་མཛོད།

༠   །གནས་ལུགས་རྟོགས་པའི་ཤེས་རབ་མི་ལྡན་ན།
    །ངེས་འབྱུང་བྱང་ཆུབ་སེམས་ལ་གོམས་བྱས་ཀྱང་།
    །སྲིད་པའི་རྩ་བ་བཅད་པར་མི་ནུས་པས།
    །དེ་ཕྱིར་རྟེན་འབྲེལ་རྟོགས་པའི་ཐབས་ལ་འབད།

༡༠   །གང་ཞིག་འཁོར་འདས་ཆོས་རྣམས་ཐམས་ཅད་ཀྱི།
    །རྒྱུ་འབྲས་ནམ་ཡང་བསླུ་བ་མེད་མཐོང་ཞིང་།
    །དམིགས་པའི་གཏད་སོ་གང་ཡིན་ཀུན་ཞིག་པ།
    །དེ་ནི་སངས་རྒྱས་དགྱེས་པའི་ལམ་ལ་ཞུགས།

༡༡   །སྣང་བ་རྟེན་འབྲེལ་བསླུ་བ་མེད་པ་དང་།
    །སྟོང་པ་ཁས་ལེན་བྲལ་བའི་གོ་བ་གཉིས།
    །ཇི་སྲིད་སོ་སོར་སྣང་བ་དེ་སྲིད་དུ།
    །དགུང་ཐུབ་པའི་དགོངས་པ་རྟོགས་པ་མེད།

༡༢ །ནམ་ཞིག་རེས་འཇོག་མེད་པར་ཅིག་ཆར་དུ།
།རྟེན་འབྲེལ་མི་བསྒྱུར་མཐོང་བ་ཙམ་ཉིད་ནས།
།ངེས་ཤེས་ཡུལ་གྱི་འཛིན་སྟངས་ཀུན་འཇིག་ན།
།དེ་ཚེ་ལྟ་བའི་དཔྱད་པ་རྫོགས་པ་ལགས།

༡༣ །གཞན་ཡང་སྣང་བས་ཡོད་མཐའ་སེལ་བ་དང་།
།སྟོང་པས་མེད་མཐའ་སེལ་ཞིང་སྟོང་པ་ཉིད།
།རྒྱུ་དང་འབྲས་བུར་འཆར་བའི་ཚུལ་ཤེས་ན།
།མཐར་འཛིན་ལྟ་བས་འཕྲོག་པར་མི་འགྱུར་རོ།

༡༤ །དེ་ལྟར་ལམ་གྱི་གཙོ་བོ་རྣམ་གསུམ་གྱི།
།གནད་རྣམས་རང་གིས་ཇི་བཞིན་རྟོགས་པའི་ཚེ།
།དབེན་པ་བསྟེན་ཏེ་བརྩོན་འགྲུས་སྟོབས་བསྐྱེད་ནས།
།གཏན་གྱི་འདུན་མ་མྱུར་དུ་སྒྲུབས་ཤིག་བུ།།

།།ཞེས་པ་འདི་ནི་མང་དུ་ཐོས་པའི་དགེ་སློང་བློ་བཟང་གྲགས་པའི་དཔལ་གྱིས་ཚ་ཁོ་དཔོན་པོ་ངག་དབང་གྲགས་པ་ལ་གདམས་པའོ།། །།

NOTES

ABBREVIATION

P: *Tibetan Tripiṭaka* (Tokyo-Kyoto: Tibetan Tripitaka Research Foundation, 1956)

INTRODUCTION

1. The Indian master Shantideva lived in the monastic university of Nalanda during the eighth century. To others he appeared quite unaccomplished and they said he only knew three things: how to eat, sleep and defecate. In an attempt to humiliate him he was designated to teach before a large gathering. To everyone's amazement he showed himself to be a very great master by teaching his guide to the Bodhisattva's way of life, *Engaging in the Bodhisattva Deeds* (*Bodhisattvacaryāvatāra, Byang chub sems dpa'i spyod pa la 'jug pa*, P5272, Vol. 99) and by displaying miraculous feats. His other extant work, *The Compendium of Training* (*Sikṣāsamuccaya, bSlabs pa kun las btus pa*, P5272, Vol. 102), is a compilation and elucidation of sutra passages about the training of Bodhisattvas. English translations: *A Guide to the Bodhisattva's Way of Life*, Stephen Batchelor, trans. (Dharamsala: Library of Tibetan Works and Archives, 1979); *The Bodhicaryāvatāra*, Kate Crosby and Andrew Skilton, trans. (Oxford: Oxford University Press, 1995); *A Guide to the Bodhisattva Way of Life*, Vesna A. Wallace and B. Alan Wallace, trans. (Ithaca: Snow Lion Publications, 1997).

2. The word *dal 'byor*, which occurs in the Tibetan translation of Shantideva's words, refers not to any human life but to one of freedom (*dal ba*) and fortune (*'byor ba*). Freedom in this context means to be free from eight adverse conditions. Four of these are non-human states as hell-beings, animals, hungry ghosts and celestial beings with extremely long lives. The suffering of those in the bad states of rebirth is so intense that they cannot think about spiritual practice. Celestial beings with long lives are absorbed in sensual pleasures or the pleasure of concentration and cannot develop an aversion to cyclic existence. Their bodies and minds are not suitable as a basis for vows of any kind.

There are four human states which prevent spiritual practice, the most serious of which is holding wrong views such as that there are no past and future lives and that there is no connection between actions and their effects. Being born a barbarian in a remote place where there is no access to Buddhist teachings, being born at a time when a Buddha's teachings do not exist in the world, and having defective faculties are also serious impediments.

Fortune means enjoying conducive conditions. Five kinds of such fortune are personal: being born as a human; being born in a place where the teachings exist and there are ordained men and women; possessing healthy faculties; not having created any seriously negative actions like the five extremely grave and the five almost as grave actions; and having faith in spiritual teachers, the three kinds of training and the texts which contain instructions on them. Five kinds of good fortune are circumstantial: that a Buddha has come to the world; that he has lit the lamp of the teachings; that these teachings are alive insofar as there are people who hear, think about and meditate on them; that there are those who can be looked upon as role-models because of their exemplary practice of the teachings; and that support and encouragement for practitioners are available.

3. The Kadampa (bKa' gdams pa) tradition was founded by Dromtön Gyelway Jungnay ('Brom ston rGyal ba'i 'byung gnas, 1004-1064), a lay practitioner and the main Tibetan disciple of the Indian master Atisha, who was invited to teach in Tibet in 1042. The Kadampa masters were known for their down-to-earth approach to practice, which they presented according to the three levels of capacity explained in Atisha's *Lamp for the Path to Enlightenment*. They laid great emphasis in public on the practice of sutra and kept their personal practice of tantra hidden. They regarded all of the Buddha's words (*bka'*) as actual instructions (*gdams*) for practice.

4. The Indian master Dharmakirti (Chos kyi grags pa) lived in the seventh century. He wrote seven treatises on valid cognition, among them his famous *Commentary on (Dignaga's) "Compendium of Valid Cog-*

nition" (Pramāṇavārttika, Tshad ma rnam 'grel, P5709, Vol. 130), in which he defines the criteria for valid perception, valid scriptural statements and valid persons.

5. Tsang (gTsang) lies in the west of central Tibet. The principal town of this area is Shigatse (gZhi ka rtse), near which is Tashi Lhünpo Monastery (bKra shis lhun po), seat of the Pänchen lamas.

6. Wölka ('Ol kha) is situated in the Loka (lHo kha) region of central Tibet.

7. Lodrak (lHo brag) is the southern part of what is now the Tibet Autonomous Region and lies on the southern shore of the lake Yardrok Yumtso (Yar 'brog g.yu mtsho).

8. Buddhapalita flourished in south India around 470-540? C.E. He studied under Samgharakshita. The book he holds in Tsongkhapa's dream is his *Commentary on Nagarjuna's Treatise on the Middle Way, (Buddhapālitamūlamadhyamakavṛtti, dBu ma rtsa ba'i 'grel pa buddha pa li ta*, P5254, Vol. 95).

9. For further information about Tsongkhapa, see *Life and Teachings of Tsong Khapa*, edited by Robert Thurman (Dharamsala, India: Library of Tibetan Works and Archives, 1982).

10. *Lam gyi gtso bo rnam gsum*, P6087, Vol. 153.

11. People are motivated by different intentions when they practice the Buddha's teachings. Practice of his teachings is considered authentic from a Buddhist point of view when it is motivated at least by the wish to gain a good rebirth. A practitioner of the initial level engages in practices which make this possible. A practitioner of the intermediate level is concerned with personal liberation from all rebirth within cyclic existence as a result of actions underlain by disturbing attitudes and emotions, and engages in practices which lead to such freedom. A practitioner of the highest level is motivated by the altruistic intention to become enlightened for the sake of all living beings and does what is necessary to become a fully enlightened Buddha. Even if from the outset we are motivated by the wish to become fully enlightened in order to help others in the most effective way, we must still do the practices associated with the initial and intermediate levels, since the insights to which they lead form the foundation for the practices that are unique to the Great Vehicle.

12. *OM MANI PADME HUNG* is the mantra of Avalokiteshvara, the embodiment of enlightened compassion. The mantra is primarily associated with the four-armed form which holds a string of crystal prayer beads and the stem of a lotus. There are many interpretations

of this profound mantra. In Ngülchu Dharmabhadra's (dNgul chu dharma bhadra, 1772-1851) *Heart Wealth of Bodhisattvas* (*rGyal sras snying nor*), a commentary on Geshe Chekawa's (dGe bshes mChad kha ba, 1101-1175) *Seven Points for Training the Mind* (*Blo sbyong don bdun ma*), the following brief interpretation occurs: the syllable *OM* serves as an invocation. *MANI* means jewel and signifies skillful means, while *PADME* means lotus and signifies wisdom. *HUNG* is the seed syllable of enlightened mind. Avalokiteshvara combines perfected skillful means and wisdom. Thus the mantra can be interpreted as a request, "You who hold the jewel and the lotus, please look on me with compassion and bless me to become like you."

13. Non-virtuous actions (*mi dge ba'i las*), virtuous contaminated actions (*zag bcas dge ba'i las*) and unfluctuating action (*mi g.yo ba'i las*) lead to a rebirth in one of the three realms of cyclic existence. Non-virtuous actions lead to a rebirth as a hell-being, a hungry spirit or as an animal in the desire realm (*'dod khams*) and virtuous contaminated actions to a rebirth in the same realm as a human or celestial being. Unfluctuating actions result in rebirth as a celestial being in the form or formless realms (*gzugs khams, gzugs med khams*). In order to create unfluctuating action one must have attained a calmly abiding mind (*zhi gnas*). There are four concentrations (*bsam gtan*) or absorptions (*snyoms 'jug*) of the form realm, which are differentiated on the basis of the accompanying feelings. A progressive development towards neutral feeling takes place. There are seventeen abodes (*gnas*) of the form realm divided among the four concentrations.

The four absorptions of the formless realm are called limitless space (*nam mkha' mtha' yas*), limitless consciousness (*rnam shes mtha' yas*), nothingness (*ci yang med*) and the peak of cyclic existence (*srid rtse*). They are differentiated on the basis of the accompanying discrimination, which becomes less and less coarse.

14. In tantra the stage of generation (*bskyed rim*) is practiced to overcome ordinary appearances and one's clinging to them. Ordinary appearances are counteracted by imagining oneself as the deity and one's surroundings as the celestial mansion and other components of the mandala. One's clinging to such ordinary appearances is countered by strong identification with the deity. Practices during the stage of completion (*rdzogs rim*) involve focusing intense attention on the energy channels, energy winds and drops of the subtle body, particularly at the different centers, to generate great bliss. This blissful awareness is eventually used to apprehend emptiness and to produce the illusory body (*sgyu lus*).

15. Geshe Puchungwa (Phu chung gZhon nu rgyal mtshan, 1031-1106) and Geshe Chengawa (sPyan snga Tshul khrims 'bar, 1038-1103).

16. The five major fields of knowledge are the arts and crafts (*bzo rig pa*), medicine (*gso ba rig pa*), grammar (*sgra rig pa*), logic (*gtan tshigs rig pa*) and Buddhist philosophy (*nang don rig pa*).

17. The five kinds of higher knowledge are knowledge of miraculous feats (*rdzu 'phrul gyi mngon shes*), the divine eye (*lha'i mig gi mngon shes*), the divine ear (*lha'i rna ba'i mngon shes*), knowledge of others' thoughts (*gzhan sems shes pa'i mngon shes*), and recollection of past lives (*gnas rjes dran gyi mngon shes*).

18. There are different versions of these eight powerful attainments. They include such powers as creating the pill (*ril bu*) which taken daily makes one radiant, strong and energetic; creating the eye ointment (*mig sman*) which makes one clairvoyant and able to see hidden treasure; the ability to travel underground (*sa 'og*), through which one can reach the treasure; the ability to travel to distant places by holding on to a sword (*ral gri*); the ability to fly in the sky (*nam mkha' la 'phur ba*) like a bird; the power to overcome sickness (*nad bcom pa*) by taking the essence of flowers or minerals; the power to cover vast distances by means of the fleet foot (*rkang mgyogs*), and the power of invisibility (*mi snang ba*).

19. *Lamp for the Path to Enlightenment* (*Bodhipathapradipa, Byang chub lam gyi sgron ma*, P5343, Vol. 103) is the forerunner of the subsequent "lam rim" literature which explains the stages of the path to enlightenment with strong emphasis on practice. Atisha (982-1054) was born into a royal family probably in what is now Bengal. Owing to his parents' opposition he had difficulty disengaging himself from royal life, but eventually, after a number of attempts, succeeded and became ordained. He studied with a hundred and fifty-seven spiritual masters but was always very moved when he recalled Dharmakirti of Suvarnadvipa, the master of the Golden Isles. Atisha made a perilous thirteen-month sea journey to Indonesia to study with this master, with whom he remained for twelve years and to whom he attributed his development of the altruistic intention. After his return to India he lived in the monastic university of Vikramashila from where he was invited to Tibet. English translation and commentary: Geshe Sonam Rinchen and Ruth Sonam, *Atisha's Lamp for the Path to Enlightenment* (Ithaca, New York: Snow Lion Publications, 1997).

20. *Lam rim chen mo*, P6001, Vol. 125.

Prologue

1. The lineage of extensive deeds (*rgya chen spyod brgyud*), coming from Maitreya and Asanga, lays emphasis on the skillful means taught by the Buddha. The lineage of the profound view (*zab mo lta brgyud*),

coming from Manjushri and Nagarjuna, mainly emphasizes the wisdom aspect of the Buddha's teachings. The inspiring practice lineage (*nyams len byin rlabs brgyud*) from the point of view of sutra starts with the Buddha Shakyamuni and comes down through Manjushri and Shantideva, and from a tantric standpoint begins with the Buddha Vajradhara and is passed down through Tilopa, Naropa and so forth.

2.   *The Essence of Good Explanations Regarding the Interpretable and the Definitive* (*Drang nges legs bshad snying po*, P6142, Vol. 153) deals with the understanding of reality and focuses on the question of which teachings by the Buddha are to be considered as interpretable and which definitive from the standpoint of the different schools of Buddhist philosophy, particularly of the Chittamatrins and Madhyamikas. See Robert Thurman's translation and explication of this difficult work, *The Central Philosophy of Tibet* (Princeton, New Jersey: Princeton University Press, 1984).

3.   The Indian Buddhist master Chandrakirti was one of the main spiritual heirs of Nagarjuna, whose works on sutra and tantra he elucidated and propagated. He lived in the monastic university of Nalanda during the seventh century and was an accomplished practitioner. His *Supplement to the Middle Way* (*Madhyamakāvatāra, dBu ma la 'jug pa*, P5261, P5262, Vol. 98) is a commentary on the meaning of Nagarjuna's *Treatise on the Middle Way* (*Madhyamakaśāstra, dBu ma'i bstan bcos*, P5224, Vol. 95), also called *Fundamental Wisdom* (*rTsa shes*), which it supplements with regard to the extensive aspect of practice. It deals with the ten Bodhisattva stages.

4.   When the Buddha Shakyamuni came to our world from the Tushita pure land (dGa' ldan yid dga' chos 'dzin), Maitreya took over as its spiritual ruler. He will eventually manifest in this world as the next Buddha and display the deeds of a supreme emanation body (*mchog gi sprul sku*). It is said that if one hears and thinks about the five treatises, which he revealed to Asanga, one will be reborn in the Tushita pure land. In Tibet many of the largest statues were of Maitreya, who is represented sitting on a throne with his feet on the ground, ready to rise and come into the world. Just as Avalokiteshvara is the embodiment of perfect compassion, Maitreya is the embodiment of perfect love. One of Maitreya's five treatises is the *Ornament for Clear Realization* (*Abhisamayālaṃkāra, mNgon par rtogs pa'i rgyan*, P5184, Vol. 88), a Mahayana text containing instructions on the hidden aspect of the Perfection of Wisdom sutras. The fact that there are twenty-one Indian commentaries on this work and many others by Tibetan masters indicates its great importance. Its subject-matter served as the basis for all the later Tibetan literature on the stages of the path.

5. The three kinds of understanding are knowledge of the bases (*gzhi shes*), knowledge of the paths (*lam shes*) and omniscience (*rnam mkhyen*). Knowledge of the bases is possessed by exalted Hearers, exalted Solitary Realizers and exalted Buddhas. The exalted are those who have gained direct understanding of reality. Exalted practitioners of the Lesser Vehicle are the main holders posited for this knowledge of the bases, referred to in the homage as the "knowledge of all" (*kun shes*). The method they employ is the direct understanding of the selflessness (*bdag med rtogs pa'i shes rab*) of all bases—the aggregates (*phung po*), constituents (*khams*) and sources (*skye mched*). The result they attain through this is liberation.

Knowledge of the paths is possessed by exalted Mahayana practitioners and exalted Buddhas, but exalted Mahayana practitioners are the main holders posited for this knowledge. The method they employ is the understanding that specifically the paths of Hearers, Solitary Realizers and the Great Vehicle as well as all else lacks true existence (*bden med rtogs pa'i shes rab*). This understanding is accompanied by special skillful means (*thabs khyad par can*). As a result they attain the ability to fulfill the needs of those with any of the three kinds of disposition.

Omniscience is possessed by Buddhas, who alone hold this form of knowledge. It is an ultimate or perfected understanding (*mthar thug pa'i ye shes*) that directly and simultaneously perceives all phenomena both in their diversity (*ji snyed pa*) and as they actually are (*ji lta ba*), and it enables them to turn the wheel of the teachings. "Diverse" in the homage refers to the many different teachings which enlightened ones give, both those to be taken literally and those which require interpretation. "All aspects" conveys the range of the topics covered and that the teachings encompass the two truths—the conventional and ultimate.

6. Geshe Potowa (Po to ba Rin chen gsal, 1031-1105) entered Reting Monastery (Rwa sgreng) in 1058 and later became its abbot for a short time. He was mainly active in Penyul ('Phan yul) and is said to have had two thousand disciples. He taught the six great texts which form the basis of the Kadampa tradition: Shantideva's *Compendium of Training* (*bSlab btus*) and *Engaging in the Bodhisattva Deeds* (*sPyod 'jug*); Asanga's *Bodhisattva Stages* (*Byang sa*); Maitreya's *Ornament for the Mahayana Sutras* (*mDo sde'i rgyan*); *Stories of the Buddha's Lives* (*sKyes rab*) by Aryashura and *The Collection* (*Tshoms*) of sutra statements.

7. Maitreya's *Ornament for the Mahayana Sutras* (*Mahāyānasūtrālaṃkāra, Theg pa chen po'i mdo sde'i rgyan*, P5521, Vol. 108) consists of twenty-one chapters which deal mainly with Mahayana conduct and present the

Chittamatrin view. The text seeks to establish the authenticity of the
Mahayana sutras as the words of the Buddha.

8.   The individual liberation vow (*so thar gyi sdom pa*) is so called because observing it enables an individual to attain liberation. It focuses
mainly on the maintenance of pure physical and verbal conduct. Different forms of this vow are taken by lay and ordained people.

The Bodhisattva vow (*byang sems kyi sdom pa*) entails restraint from
eighteen major and forty-six minor transgressions. Ideally it is taken
when one wishes and feels ready to engage in the deeds of Bodhisattvas. Emphasis is placed not only on physical and verbal conduct but
on constantly maintaining an altruistic state of mind towards all living
beings.

The tantric vow (*gsang sngags kyi sdom pa*) consists of restraint from
fourteen general transgressions. There are also numerous pledges and
commitments which must be kept. One is required to observe the tantric
vow after receiving yoga tantra and highest yoga tantra empowerments.

9.   The teachings on discipline (*'dul ba'i sde snod*) mainly set forth the
training in ethical discipline (*tshul khrims kyi bslab pa*) or conduct (*spyod
pa*). The teachings on knowledge (*mngon pa'i sde snod*) primarily explain the training in wisdom (*shes rab kyi bslab pa*) or the view (*lta ba*),
while those on sutra (*mdo sde'i sde snod*) principally explain the training in meditative stabilization (*ting nge 'dzin gyi bslab pa*) or meditation
(*sgom pa*).

10.   Aryadeva was the spiritual son of Nagarjuna and was active in the
monastic university of Nalanda during the first half of the third century. His work *Four Hundred Stanzas on the Yogic Deeds of Bodhisattvas*
(*Bodhisattvayogacaryācatuhśatakaśāstra, Byang chub sems dpa'i rnal 'byor
spyod pa bzhi brgya pa'i bstan bcos*, P5246, Vol. 95) discusses the distorted
ideas and disturbing emotions which prevent true Bodhisattva activity and the attainment of enlightenment. The first eight chapters establish conventional reality, while the second eight establish ultimate
reality by refuting various misconceptions regarding, for instance, the
person, time, space and matter. English translation: Geshe Sonam
Rinchen and Ruth Sonam, *Yogic Deeds of Bodhisattvas: Gyeltsap on
Aryadeva's Four Hundred* (Ithaca: Snow Lion Publications, 1994).

11.   Milarepa (Mi la ras pa, Thos pa dga' 1040-1123) is remembered for
the many hardships he endured in his devoted efforts to receive teachings from Marpa (Mar pa lo tsa' ba Chos kyi blo gros, 1012-1097), with
whom he stayed for six years and eight months. He is remembered too
for his single-mindedness and austere life as a meditator, and for his
songs of experience. Of his many disciples the foremost were

Rechungpa (Ras chung rDo rje grags, 1083-1161) and Gampopa (sGam po pa, also known as Dvags po lha rje bSod nams rin chen, 1079-1153).

12. The Indian master Asanga (Thogs med) lived in the fourth century and was a trailblazer in establishing the Chittamatra (*sems tsam*) system of philosophical tenets, although he himself is said to have held the Prasangika-Madhyamika (*dbu ma thal 'gyur pa*) view. His *Compendium of Knowledge* (*Abhidharmasamuccaya, mNgon pa kun btus*, P5550, Vol. 112) sets out the focal objects of the paths: the aggregates, constituents and elements, the four noble truths and the twelve links of dependent arising. An extensive explanation of mind and mental activities is included. The text contains instruction on how to practice by controlling one's senses and training in ethical discipline, concentration and wisdom as well as explanation of the thirty-seven factors concordant with enlightenment. It concludes by explaining the results of these practices, through which all faults are brought to an end and the highest wisdom is attained. These topics are presented mainly from a Chittamatrin standpoint.

13. The thirty-two major physical marks (*mtshan bzang po*) denote that the person who possesses them is holy. Each of them is the result of qualities accomplished and practices performed in the past. The eighty minor marks (*dpe byed bzang po*) allow others to infer the inner qualities of those who possess them. They are listed in the eighth chapter of Maitreya's *Ornament for Clear Realization*.

14. *The Array of Trunks Sutra* (*Gaṇḍavyūhasūtra, sDong po bkod pa'i mdo*, also known as *sDong po rgyan pa'i mdo*, P761, Vol. 26) is part of the *Avataṃsakasūtra*.

15. Geshe Lhabchungwa (lHab chung ba or lHab mi Shes rab g.yung drung), Geshe Lhasowa (lHa bzo ba), Geshe Nyokmopa (Nyog mo pa) and Geshe Tölungpa (sTod lungs pa Rin chen snying po, 1032-1116) were all contemporaries of Atisha.

The tantra of the meditational deity Heruka, also known as Chakrasamvara ('Khor lo bde mchog), belongs to the mother tantra category of the highest class of tantra (*bla med rgyud*). It is particularly associated with the development of wisdom and the generation of great bliss.

16. Dharmakirti of Suvarnadvipa (gSer gling pa Chos kyi grags pa) was a member of the royal family during the Shailendra Empire. He is known as the master of "the Golden Isles." This term was used to refer to Sumatra, Java and the islands of the eastern archipelago. He enjoyed considerable stature as a teacher and exponent of Buddhism and had other Indian students besides Atisha. He certainly visited India and spent some time studying there.

17. Naktso Lotsawa (Nak tsho lo tsa ba Tshul khrims rgyal ba, 1011-?) travelled to India twice, the second time in 1037 to invite Atisha. He was his student for nineteen years and wrote an eighty-verse praise recounting Atisha's life-story. Gompa Rinchen Lama (sGom pa Rin chen bla ma), Khutön (Khu ston brTson 'grus g.yung drung, 1011-1075) and Kawa Shakya Wangchuk (Ka ba Shakya dbang phyug) all became disciples of Atisha soon after he arrived in Tibet.

18. Nyanang (gNya' nang) is a southwestern area of what is now the Tibet Autonomous Region. Its southern part borders on Nepal.

19. Pänchen Losang Chökyi Gyeltsen (Pan chen Blo bzang chos kyi rgyal mtshan, 1570-1662) was the first Pänchen Lama, and his influence had a wide-reaching effect on the Gelugpa (dGe lugs pa) tradition founded by Tsongkhapa. He was the author of *The Comfortable Path* (*Lam rim bde lam*) and *Offerings to the Spiritual Teacher* (*Bla ma mchod pa*), which are still widely studied and practiced today. The Pänchen Lamas are considered to be emanations of Amitayus.

20 Trungpa Gyeltsap (Drung pa rgyal tsab Blo bzang brtson 'grus rgyal mtshan) lived in the seventeenth century and was born into a royal family whose territory was seized by the king of Ladakh (La dwags). Trungpa Gyeltsap was taken prisoner and threatened with death but showed no signs of fear. He had wanted to become ordained even before these events and when he was eventually released, he took the vows of a novice and of a fully ordained monk from Pänchen Losang Chökyi Gyeltsen.

21. Sakya Jetsün Trakpa Gyeltsen (Sa skya rje btsun Grags pa rgyal mtshan, 1147-1216) was the uncle and mentor of the famous Sakyapandita (Sa skya pandita Kun dga' rgyal tshan, 1184-1251). The latter was the first Tibetan to be given the title "pandita," which he received at the age of twenty because of his extensive learning. He took full ordination at twenty-seven. Of the many books he wrote, his *Classification of the Three Vows* (*sDom gsum rab dbye*) and his *Precious Treasure of Good Explanations* (*Legs bshad rin po che'i gter*) are among the best known. He played a significant role in establishing relations with Mongolia and China.

22. Lha Lama Jangchup Wö (lHa bla ma Byang chub 'od, 984-1078) belonged to the royal dynasty of Guge-Purang (Gu ge Pu hrang), which descended from the ancient Yarlung (Yar lung) monarchy. By the end of the tenth century their territory stretched from Ladakh to Purang and included all of western Tibet, which in ancient times was known as Zhang-Zhung. Lha Lama Jangchup Wö took ordination in 1023 and ascended the secular throne of Guge left vacant by the death of his older brother.

23. *Sañchayagāthāprajñāpāramitāsūtra, Shes rab kyi pha rol tu phyin pa mdo sdud pa*, P735, Vol. 49.

24. Hearers (*snyan thos*) and Solitary Realizers (*rang sangs rgyas*) are intent on gaining personal liberation. They are practitioners of the Hinayana or Lesser Vehicle (*theg dman pa*), so called because their objective is limited to their own well-being. Practitioners of the Mahayana or Great Vehicle (*theg chen pa*), also referred to as practitioners of the Bodhisattva Vehicle, aspire to attain complete enlightenment for the sake of all beings and therefore have a greater objective. Solitary Realizers accumulate more merit over a longer period than Hearers and do not depend upon the instructions of a spiritual teacher in their last rebirth before they attain liberation and become Foe Destroyers (*dgra bcom pa*). Foe Destroyers are those who have vanquished the foe of the disturbing emotions and put an end to their cyclic existence by uprooting ignorance.

25. The Perfection of Wisdom sutras were taught by the Buddha at Vulture's Peak outside Rajgir. As an act of homage to the teaching he was about to give he prepared his own seat. The explicit subject-matter (*dngos don*) of these sutras consists of the stages of the profound paths of practice regarding the nature of reality, the emptiness of intrinsic existence of all phenomena, and how this understanding is used to eliminate the obstructions to liberation and to knowledge of all phenomena. The hidden subject-matter (*sbas don*) consists of the stages of the extensive paths of practice, namely everything which constitutes the development of skillful means. Normally a hidden subject-matter is found only in the tantras, while sutras may have an explicit (*dngos don*) and implicit subject-matter (*shugs don*). The fact that the Perfection of Wisdom sutras have a hidden subject-matter places them close to the tantras regarding the subtlety of their content. They contain much that can only be understood with the help of a spiritual teacher's instructions. Of the many versions of these sutras the best known in the Tibetan canon are those consisting of a hundred thousand verses, twenty thousand verses, eight thousand verses and the *Heart Sutra* (*Bhagavatiprajñāpāramitāhṛdayasūtra, bCom ldan 'das ma shes rab kyi pha rol tu phyin pa'i snying po'i mdo*, P160, Vol. 6), the most condensed Perfection of Wisdom sutra.

THE WISH FOR FREEDOM

1. Such a body and mind are referred to as *nyer len gyi phung po*. There are five groups or aggregates (*phung po*)—forms, feelings, discriminations, compositional factors (such as secondary mental activities), and

different kinds of consciousness. These five aggregates constitute body and mind. *Nyer len* is a contraction of *nyer ba len pa*, meaning "to acquire." It indicates that these aggregates have been acquired through disturbing emotions and contaminated actions. It also indicates that this body and mind will lead to the acquisition of further contaminated aggregates in future rebirths.

When we are about to die, we are unwilling to let go of our body and attachment to the self manifests. An attraction to the next rebirth arises which triggers an imprint left by a previous action, leading to rebirth in the desire and form realms with five aggregates or in the formless realm with four aggregates. Conception takes place and the embryonic body and mind are pervaded by the seeds of contaminated actions and disturbing emotions. They are thus an instance of the pervasive suffering of conditioning.

2.   The twelve-part process of dependent arising (*rten 'brel yan lag bcu gnyis*) is normally presented in the following order: ignorance (*ma rigs pa*), formative action (*'du byed*), consciousness (*rnam par shes pa*), name and form (*ming gzugs*), the sources (*skyed mched*), contact (*reg pa*), feeling (*tshor ba*), craving (*sred pa*), grasping (*len pa*), existence (*srid pa*), birth (*skye ba*), ageing and death (*rga shi*).

3.   Geshe Sharawa (Sha ra ba, also Shar ba pa, 1070-1141) was ordained by Geshe Potowa and had more than three thousand students, many of whom came to him after the great master Potowa passed away. He is said to have memorized the Tibetan canon of the Buddha's sutras. He had good knowledge of Sanskrit and supervised revisions of earlier translations with which he was not satisfied. He taught the essentials of how to transform one's way of thinking to Geshe Chekawa (mChad kha ba, 1101-1175), who later wrote the famous text *Seven Points for Training the Mind (Blo byong don bdun ma)*.

4.   It is said that *Parting from the Four Attachments (Zhen pa bzhi bral)* is a teaching originally imparted by Manjushri to Sachen Kunga Nyingpo (Sa chen Kun dga' snying po, 1092-1158). These quintessential instructions refer to Jetsün Trakpa Gyeltsen's commentary on the teaching.

5.   Shang Nachung Tönpa (Zhang sNa chung ston pa) lived in the eleventh century. He had particularly extensive knowledge of the teachings of Maitreya and Asanga.

6.   The Indian Buddhist master Nagarjuna (Klu sgrub, first to second century) was the trailblazer who established the Madhyamika system of philosophical tenets. His *Letter to a Friend (Suhṛllekha, bShes pa'i spring yig*, P5682, Vol. 129) addresses advice to his friend, a king of the Satavahana dynasty which ruled over a vast area of India including

much of modern Madhya Pradesh, Maharashtra, Andhra Pradesh, part of south Orissa and part of Karnataka. In Tibetan literature this king is referred to by the name of bDe spyod bzang po. In *Letter to a Friend* Nagarjuna discusses concisely and in detail the practices associated with the three different levels of capacity. His explanation is directed towards both householders and the ordained.

7. Lingrepa (gLing ras Pad ma rdo rje, 1128-1188) was a lay practitioner and disciple of Pagmo Drupa (Phag mo gru rDo rje rgyal po, 1110-1170). The Drukpa Kagyu ('Brug pa bKa' brgyud) line originated from Lingrepa.

8. Yang Gönpa (Yang dgon pa rGyal mtshan dpal, 1213-1258) was born into a family of Nyingma (rNying ma) practitioners, many of whom had been highly accomplished. He displayed extraordinary qualities such as clairvoyance from an early age. His teacher Götsangpa (rGod tshang pa mGon po rdo rje, 1189-1258) travelled widely, practicing wherever he went. Among the places he visited were Mt. Kailash, Jalandhara in the lower Kangra Valley in Himalayan India and Tsari (Tsa ri) in southern Tibet towards the border with Assam, a place of pilgrimage sacred to Heruka, where he served others in retreat. He had many distinguished disciples.

9. The Great Completion (*rdzogs pa chen po*) involves the highest practices of tantra and consists of making manifest present pristine awareness (*rig pa*) which is free from stains, luminous, clear and bare of all obstructions. Since all appearances associated with cyclic existence and nirvana are contained within this, it is called "completion," and because there is no superior means to freedom from cyclic existence it is called "great."

10. Geshe Bengungyel ('Ban gung rgyal), one of the Kadampa masters, was a thief and brigand in the early part of his life. Later, after he had reformed, he used to chide himself when he noticed that he was doing or thinking anything unwholesome. He would say, "There you go again, you villain Bengungyel, still at your old ways!" But when he had done or thought something good, he would use his religious name and say, "Congratulations Geshe Tsultrim Gyelwa, keep up the good work!"

11. Many masters of the Kadampa tradition were active in Pembo ('Phan po or 'Phan yul), an area to the north of Lhasa, where they established a number of important monasteries.

12. The Tibetan New Year, calculated according to lunar cycles, normally occurs during the month of February. The pilgrims therefore left in spring.

13. This statue, known as "The Wish-fulfilling Lord" (Jo bo yid bzhin nor bu), is said to depict the Buddha Shakyamuni at the age of twelve. It was brought to Tibet by Kongjo (Kong jo), the Chinese wife of King Srongtsen Gampo (Srong btsan sgam po), who lived in the seventh century.

14. *mKha' khyab kyi ting nge 'dzin.*

15. *bKa' gdams phugs nor bcu.*

16. *Bodhisattvayogacaryācatuḥśatakaṭīkā, Byang chub sems dpa'i rnal 'byor spyod pa bzhi brgya pa'i rgya cher 'grel pa,* P5266, Vol. 98. These analogies may be found in *Yogic Deeds of Bodhisattvas, Gyel-tsap on Aryadeva's Four Hundred.*

17. *Phyi ma'i snang shas.*

18. Mention of pure lands (*dag zhing*) is found in Mahayana literature. They are described as places where conditions are in every way favorable to spiritual development. There one enjoys the inspiring company of spiritual teachers and supportive spiritual companions. The main practice which leads to rebirth in a pure land is purification of the mind.

19. These four points are the definite nature of actions (*las nges pa'i tshul*), the increasing nature of actions (*las 'phel che ba*), that one will not experience the result of an action one hasn't performed (*las ma byas pa dang mi 'phrad pa*) and that once an action has been performed it does not go to waste (*las byas pa chud mi za*).

20. Nagarjuna's *Precious Garland of Advice for the King* (*Rājapari-kathāratnāvalī, rGyal po la gtam bya ba rin po che'i phreng ba,* P5658, Vol. 129) explains both the extensive and profound paths to enlightenment, emphasizing that the root of enlightenment is the exalted understanding of reality. Like his *Letter to a Friend,* it is addressed to his friend the king of the Satavahana dynasty. The *Precious Garland* contains very practical advice, still relevant today, on how to govern in accordance with the Buddha's teaching. English translation: Jeffrey Hopkins, in Nagarjuna and the Seventh Dalai Lama's *The Precious Garland and The Song of the Four Mindfulnesses* (New York: Harper and Row, 1975); Jeffrey Hopkins, trans., *Buddhist Advice for Living and Liberation: Nāgārjuna's Precious Garland* (Ithaca: Snow Lion Publications, 1998).

21. Those who have made a formal commitment to take refuge in the Three Jewels for as long as they live observe certain precepts. The individual precepts concern what should and should not be done with regard to each of the Three Jewels. The precepts in relation to the Buddha are that one should not consider any other refuge or source of

ᅟ

protection higher than the Buddha and should respect all images of the Buddha and enlightened beings, whether or not they are well made or made of something precious.

The precepts in relation to the teachings are, as far as possible, not to harm other living beings and to respect all texts which contain instruction on what behavior and attitudes to adopt and what to discard, since they are intended for one's own and others' well-being.

The precepts in relation to the spiritual community are not to allow one's physical, verbal or mental activity to be influenced by those who dislike and oppose the Buddha's teaching and to respect all members of the spiritual community, no matter which form of Buddhism they practice, regarding them as spiritual companions, offering them material help and fostering a relationship with them based on the teachings.

The general precepts are to take refuge again and again, remembering the special qualities and distinguishing features of the Three Jewels; to offer the first and best part of food and drink and to make other offerings, remembering the kindness of the Three Jewels; to encourage others, who show an interest, to take refuge; to entrust oneself to the Three Jewels in whatever activities one undertakes; not to give up the Three Jewels even in joke or at the cost of one's life; to take refuge three times each day and three times each night, remembering the benefits of doing so: (1) one becomes a Buddhist, (2) and a suitable basis for all vows, (3) formerly accumulated karmic obstructions come to an end, (4) extensive stores of positive energy are easily accumulated, (5) harm from humans and non-humans cannot affect one, (6) one will not take bad rebirths, (7) one will accomplish all one's wishes, and (8) one will become enlightened quickly.

22. Actions which are performed but not accumulated (*byas la ma bsags pa'i las*) are physical, verbal or mental good or bad activities performed accidentally, unwillingly with regret or without any explicit motivation. Actions which are accumulated but not performed (*bsags la ma byas pa'i las*) are good or bad actions that one intends to but does not perform. For example, one might plan a robbery but not actually carry it out.

23. *sKabs gsum pa.*

24. The six kinds of suffering or drawbacks experienced in all states of cyclic existence are: uncertainty (*nges pa med pa*), being unsatisfied (*ngoms pa med pa*), giving up one's body again and again (*lus yang nas yang du 'dor ba*), repeatedly being conceived (*yang yang nying mtshams sbyor ba*), repeatedly being high and low (*yang yang mtho dman du 'gyur ba*), and being friendless (*grogs med pa*).

25. These treatises, referred to as *Sa sde lnga* in Tibetan (P55536-55543, Vols. 109-111), present the development of the different stages of insight along the path to enlightenment. Asanga approaches this development from a Chittamatrin standpoint and in these treatises deals mainly with activity rather than with philosophical view. Of these five treatises *Levels of Yogic Practice* (*Yogacaryābhūmi, rNal 'byor spyod pa'i sa*, also called *Sa'i ngos gzhi*), which forms the first three volumes of this series, contains the *Hearer Levels* (*Śrāvakabhūmi, Nyan sa*), mainly about the cultivation of a calmly abiding mind, and the *Bodhisattva Levels* (*Bodhisattvabhūmi, Byang sa*), one of the principal texts taught in the Kadampa tradition. Both these texts are frequently cited by Tsongkhapa in his *Great Exposition of the Stages of the Path*.

26. The three kinds of suffering are the suffering of pain (*sdug bsngal gyi sdug bsngal*), the suffering of change ('*gyur ba'i sdug bsngal*), and the pervasive suffering of conditioning (*khyab pa 'du byed kyi sdug bsngal*).

27. Feelings can be pleasurable, painful or neutral. Virtuous neutral feelings accompany, for example, the first preparation (*nyer bsdogs*) for the first concentration (*bsam gtan*) of the form realm, accomplished when calm abiding (*zhi gnas*) is attained. These virtuous neutral feelings are contaminated when the preparation precedes worldly paths which do not lead beyond cyclic existence but through which manifest disturbing emotions can be suppressed. The virtuous neutral feelings are uncontaminated when the first preparation acts as a basis for uncontaminated paths, associated with the wish for freedom from cyclic existence, which lead to liberation. An example of non-virtuous neutral feelings are the neutral feelings accompanying attachment to the contaminated aggregates in the desire realm. Unspecified neutral feelings are, for instance, neither virtuous nor non-virtuous neutral feelings accompanying activities such as walking, sitting and standing.

THE ALTRUISTIC INTENTION

1. *Mahāratnakūtasūtra, dKon mchog brtsegs pa'i mdo*, P.760, Vols. 22-24.

2. The altruistic intention is the only way into the Great Vehicle. When you possess it you are called a child of the Victorious Ones and outshine Hearers and Solitary Realizers in terms of your disposition. You become a supreme object of offerings, easily complete the stores of merit and insight, quickly purify previous wrong-doing and obstructions, accomplish whatever you wish, are invulnerable to harm and obstacles, swiftly complete all paths of insight and become a source of joy and happiness for living beings. These are briefly some of the benefits and advantages

of developing the altruistic intention. The *Array of Trunks Sutra* lists two hundred benefits bestowed by the altruistic intention.

3. The five paths are the path of accumulation (*tshogs lam*), the path of preparation (*sbyor lam*), the path of seeing (*mthong lam*), the path of meditation (*sgom lam*) and the path of no more learning (*mi slob lam*). One enters the Mahayana path of accumulation and becomes a Bodhisattva when the altruistic intention is spontaneously and constantly present. At this point one begins accumulating the great stores of merit and insight necessary for the attainment of enlightenment. The path of preparation, marked by the union of calm abiding and special insight focusing on emptiness, prepares one for direct perception of reality. When this experience of reality is achieved, one attains the path of seeing and the first Bodhisattva stage. On the path of meditation the practitioner gains ever-increasing familiarity with the direct perception of emptiness and practices the perfections, eliminating more and more subtle obstructions to enlightenment. When all of these have been removed, one attains the path of no more learning and becomes an enlightened being.

4. There are five deluded or bad views (*lta ngan*). The false view of the transitory collection (*'jig lta*) focuses on the validly existent self, attributed to the mental and physical aggregates which are a transitory collection. It distorts this self by assenting to its appearance as something which exists independently from the body and mind, and it holds this fabricated self to be a real "I" and "mine." This leads to attachment and aversion, the actions that express these feelings and the suffering that results from them. The false view of the transitory collection is the basis for all other bad views.

A view holding to an extreme (*mthar lta*) focuses on the self, as apprehended by the false view of the transitory collection, and regards it as permanent, in the sense of unchanging, or as subject to annihilation, in the sense of discontinuing at death. The conception of a bad view as supreme (*lta ba mchog 'dzin*) regards a wrong view of the mental and physical aggregates to be correct and unsurpassed. The conception of bad ethics and modes of conduct as supreme (*tshul khrims brtul zhugs mchog 'dzin*) considers a faulty system of ethics, a faulty mode of conduct or the states of mind and physical and verbal activities associated with these as a method of purification or of gaining liberation. It leads to fruitless effort.

Although all of the preceding are wrong views, in this context wrong views (*log lta*) specifically refers to denying what exists, such as past and future lives and the connection between actions and their effects, or to affirming as existent that which does not exist, such as a creator of the world.

5.   The seven cause and effect instructions (*rgyu 'bras man ngag bdun*) consist of recognizing all living beings as our mothers (*mar shes*), remembering their kindness (*drin dran*), cultivating the wish to repay their kindness (*drin gzo*), developing the affection which sees them as lovable (*yid 'ong byams pa*), cultivating compassion (*snying rje*), the special wish (*lhag bsam*) and the actual altruistic intention (*sems bskyed*).

6.   Equalizing and exchanging self and others (*bdag gzhan mnyam brje*) initially involves training ourselves to cherish others as much as we cherish ourselves (*bdag bzhan mnyam pa*), in that we are as much concerned about their happiness and suffering as we are about our own. We then continue by examining the faults of selfishness from many points of view (*rang gces 'dzin gyi skyon sgo du ma nas bsam pa*) and the numerous advantages of cherishing others (*gzhan gces 'dzin gyi yon tan sgo du ma nas bsam pa*) until we are able to switch our attitude entirely (*bdag gzhan brje ba'i bsam pa dngos*). Previously we have been totally concerned with ourselves and have neglected others. Now our concern is focused entirely on their well-being and we forget about ourselves. To strengthen love which wishes to give others happiness and compassion which wishes to alleviate their suffering we do the practice of giving and taking (*gtong len*). Shantideva explains in detail how to bring about these radical changes in his chapter on concentration in *Engaging in the Bodhisattva Deeds*.

7.   *Illumination of the Thought, Extensive Explanation of (Chandrakirti's) "Supplement to the Middle Way,"* dBu ma la 'jug pa'i rgya cher bshad pa dgongs pa rab gsal, P6143, Vol. 154. English translation of first five chapters: Jeffrey Hopkins, *Compassion in Tibetan Buddhism* (Ithaca: Snow Lion Publications, 1980). Sixth chapter: Anne Carolyn Klein, *Path to the Middle: Oral Mādhyamika Philosophy in Tibet* (Albany: State University of New York Press, 1994).

8.   *Lam rim bsdus don / Byang chub lam gyi rim pa'i nyams len gyi rnam gzhag mdor bsdus*, the *Collected Works of Rje Tsoṅ-kha-pa Blo-bzaṅ-grags-pa*, Vol. kha, *thor bu*, 65b.2-68b.1 (New Delhi: Ngawang Gelek Demo, 1975). For an English translation of the verses by Ruth Sonam, see "The Abridged Stages of the Path to Enlightenment" in *Chö Yang* No. 7 (Sidhpur: Norbulingka Institute, 1996).

9.   The precepts for safeguarding the altruistic intention in this life are to think repeatedly about its many benefits as a source of inspiration; to strengthen it by consciously arousing it three times during the day

and three times during the night; to create a strong store of positive energy to prevent it from declining; and never to give up even a single living being. To insure that we will also have the altruistic intention in future lives, we practice restraint from four black or negative activities and cultivate four white or positive ones.

The first black action is intentionally to deceive the abbot who has ordained us, our spiritual teacher who gives us teaching and who may also support us materially or those who possess qualities which make them worthy of offerings. The second is to cause someone who is happy about what they have done or are doing for others to regret their good action. The third is to speak disparagingly to others about someone who is practicing the Great Vehicle in a correct and sincere way. The fourth is to behave towards others with dissimulation and deceit out of an impure intention.

The four white actions counteract the black ones. The first is never, even at the cost of one's life or just as a joke, to deceive any living being. The second is to be honest and sincere in all our dealings with others. The third is to see them as our teachers and cultivate pure perception of them, particularly of Bodhisattvas. The fourth is to encourage those over whom we exercise some influence to enter not the Lesser Vehicle but the Great Vehicle because its teachings are the most comprehensive.

10. The Bodhisattva vow is the commitment to practice the ethical discipline of a Bodhisattva and specifically to refrain from eighteen main and forty-six secondary infractions. The Indian master Chandragomin discusses these in his *Twenty Verses on the Bodhisattva Vow* (*Bodhisattvasamvaravimśaka, Byang chub sems dpa'i sdom pa nyi shu pa*, P5582. Vol. 114), see forthcoming translation and commentary by Geshe Sonam Rinchen and Ruth Sonam, *The Bodhisattva Vow* (Ithaca: Snow Lion Publications, forthcoming).

THE CORRECT VIEW

1. The view of the Middle Way (*dbu ma'i lta ba*), expounded by the Buddha in the Perfection of Wisdom sutras and elucidated by Nagarjuna, Aryadeva, Chandrakirti and their followers, is that things are neither ultimately existent nor conventionally non-existent. Their status is between these two, in that they lack true or objective existence but exist conventionally as mere appearances and attributions made by conceptuality and language.

2. *Samādhirājasūtra, Ting nge 'dzin rgyal po'i mdo*, P795, Vol. 31-32.

3. *Vimalakīrtinirdeśasūtra, Dri ma med par grags pas bstan pa'i mdo*, P843, Vol. 34.

4. The wisdom truth body (*ye shes chos sku*) of an enlightened being results mainly from the great store of insight and embodies complete personal development. It is perceived only by other enlightened beings. The form bodies (*gzugs sku*) result primarily from the great store of merit and consist of the enjoyment (*longs sku*) and emanation (*sprul sku*) bodies. These are manifestations of enlightened form for the benefit of others. The enjoyment body teaches continually and is perceived only by exalted beings. Emanation bodies are perceived by all those with the karmic predispositions to do so.

5. *Triskandhakasūtra, Phung bo gsum pa'i mdo*, P950, Vol. 37.

6. In this context a mandala is a representation of the universe and everything precious within it offered as a gift to all those in whom one takes refuge, such as one's spiritual teachers, meditational deities, Buddhas and Bodhisattvas. The representation may be created on a round base, commonly made of copper or silver, on which heaps of rice or grain, which may be colored with a natural dye, are placed within three rings, stacked one on top of the other. As each handful of rice representing different elements of the universe is added, the appropriate words are recited. Shells, beads and semi-precious or precious jewels are often mixed with the rice. However, if one does not possess such things, very simple materials may also be used, since offering the mandala is primarily an act of imagination. The universe can also be represented by a hand gesture which is made while reciting the verses. In certain practices one imagines the various parts of one's body becoming the different elements which make up the universe to be offered.

7. There are many versions of this seven-part practice (*yan lag bdun pa*). The words are intended to help the practitioner perform the seven activities which create positive energy and purify wrong-doing, the necessary basis for all other practices. Homage or obeisance (*phyag 'tshal ba*) is made to Buddhas, Bodhisattvas and all noble beings who are our inspiration. We then make actual and imagined gifts to them (*mchod pa phul ba*), acknowledge our wrong-doing (*bshags pa phul ba*), rejoice (*rjes su yi rang ba*) in our own and others' virtue, request (*bskul ba*) the enlightened ones to teach in order to dispel the darkness of ignorance, supplicate (*gsol ba 'debs pa*) them not to pass away but to remain in the world to which they bring light, and dedicate (*bsngo ba*) our merit in general and specifically that which is created through the performance of this practice to the peace, happiness and complete enlightenment of all living beings.

8. The proponents of the four schools of Buddhist philosophical tenets are the Vaibhashikas (*bye brag smra ba*), the Sautrantikas (*mdo sde pa*), the Chittamatrins (*sems tsam pa*) and the Madhyamikas (*dbu ma*

pa), consisting of the Svatantrikas (*rang rgyud pa*) and the Prasangikas (*thal 'gyur pa*). See Geshe Lhundup Sopa and Jeffery Hopkins, *Cutting Through Appearances: Practice and Theory of Tibetan Buddhism* (Ithaca, New York: Snow Lion Publications, 1989) for a succinct presentation of these systems of thought.

9. To illustrate the notion of a self-sufficient substantially existent self (*rang rkya thub pa'i rdzas su yod pa'i bdag*) and its relationship to the aggregates the analogy of a king and his court is used. The king is not independent of the court but has authority over it. The analogy of a carrier and his load is also used. For Sautrantikas the object of refutation is the absence of such a substantially existent self which can be apprehended other than in dependence on the aggregates.

10. One section of the Chittamatrin school, known as the followers of scripture—mainly followers of Asanga—posit eight kinds of consciousness: the five kinds of sense consciousness (*dbang shes*), mental consciousness (*yid shes*), foundational consciousness (*kun gzhi*) and afflicted mind (*nyon yid*). Afflicted mind mainly consists of misconceptions of the self. Foundational consciousness, which is unobstructed and neutral, carries the imprints of past virtuous and non-virtuous actions.

11. According to the commentary on *The Three Principal Aspects of the Path* (see Source Readings) by Sherap Gyatso (Shes rab rgya mtsho, 19th century), the fifty-seventh throne-holder of Tashi Kyil Monastery (bKra shis 'khyil) in Amdo, the Indian master Bhavaviveka asserts that without the focal mainstay (*dmigs pa'i gtad so*) of intrinsic existence (*rang gi mtshan nyid kyis grub pa*) all presentations of the connection between actions and their effects would collapse and everything would be non-existent. For him intrinsic existence is the fundamental premise in relation to which one can investigate whether a pot or a rabbit's horn exists. Chandrakirti, on the other hand, says that with such a mainstay or basic premise, no matter how much one speaks about the absence of true existence, the remnants of the conception of true existence persist because the object of negation has not been refuted. Since the notion of objective existence would still be present, things could only exist in and of themselves and could in no way be said to have mere nominal existence.

12. Although sometimes attributed to Geshe Dolpa (Dol pa), this well-known Kadampa saying (*mig rgyang bsring blo rgya bskyed khong gsang lhod*) is more frequently attributed to Gompa Rinchen Lama.

13. Tsako Wönpo Ngawang Drakpa (Tsha kho dbon po Ngag dbang grags pa) was born into a ruling family of Tsako in Gyamo Rong (rGya mo rong) in eastern Tibet. He made the long journey to central Tibet

where he studied with many great masters before he met Tsongkhapa. The *Three Principal Aspects of the Path* was written for this close disciple. Ngawang Drakpa acted as Tsongkhapa's attendant and travelled with him from monastery to monastery. He received teachings on the stages of the path, tantric empowerments and instructions on the stages of generation and completion from Tsongkhapa and he quickly attained profound insights. Together they performed many fasting retreats (*smyung gnas*) devoted to Avalokiteshvara and both made fervent prayers of aspiration. There were many signs that Ngawang Drakpa would accomplish much later in life. When he eventually returned to Domay (mDo smad), the part of eastern Tibet where he was born, he founded a number of monasteries to propagate Tsongkhapa's teachings.

14. Pabongka Rinpoche (Pha bong kha rin po che, Byams pa bstan 'dzin 'phrin las rgya mtsho, also known to his disciples as Bla ma bDe chen snying po, 1878-1941) was an eminent Gelugpa master and the foremost spiritual teacher of His Holiness the fourteenth Dalai Lama's junior tutor, Kyabje Trijang Rinpoche (sKyabs rje Khri byang rin po che Blo bzang ye shes, 1901-1981). The text *Opening up the Good Path: Notes on the Oral Commentary Given When the Glorious and Good Vajradhara Pabongka Bestowed the Profound Teachings on the Principal Paths (rDo rje 'chang Pha bong kha dpal bzang pos lam gtso'i zab khrid skabs kyi gsung bshad zin bris lam bzang sgo 'byed)* compiled by Lobsang Dorje (Blo bzang rdo rje) has been translated under the title *Tsongkhapa: The Principal Teachings of Buddhism* by Geshe Lobsang Tharchin with Michael Roach in the Classics of Middle Asia series (Howell: Mahayana Sutra and Tantra Press, 1989).

Source Readings

Tibetan commentaries that served as a basis for the teaching:

rDo rje 'chang Pha bong kha dpal bzang pos lam gtso'i zab khrid skabs kyi gsung bshad zin bris lam bzang sgo 'byed, notes by Blo bzang rdo rje based on the teachings by Pha bong kha Byams pa bstan 'dzin 'phrin las rgya mtsho (1878-1941)

Lam gyi gtso bo rnam gsum gyi khri yig lam bzang gsal ba'i sgron ma by Tshe mchog gling yongs 'dzin Ye shes rgyal mtshan (1713-1793)

Lam gyi gtso bo rnam gsum gyi 'grel pa 'dod 'jo'i dpag bsam by bsTan dar lha rams pa (1759-?)

Lam gtso'i zin tho blo gter pad mo rgyas pa'i nyin byed by Shes rab rgya mtsho (1803-1875)

An English translation of the above-mentioned notes on Pha bong ka Rin po che's teaching:

Tsongkhapa: the Principal Teachings of Buddhism by Geshe Lobsang Tharchin with Michael Roach in the Classics of Middle Asia series (Howell: Mahayana Sutra and Tantra Press, 1989)